CITY AGAINST SUBURB

CITY AGAINST SUBURB

The Culture Wars in an American Metropolis

Joseph A. Rodriguez

Westport, Connecticut
London

Library of Congress Cataloging-in-Publication Data

Rodriguez, Joseph A., 1958–
    City against suburb : the culture wars in an American metropolis /
Joseph A. Rodriguez.
        p.   cm.
    Includes bibliographical references and index.
    ISBN 0–275–96406–X (alk. paper)
    1. San Francisco Bay Area (Calif.)—Social conditions.
    2. Sociology, Urban—California—San Francisco Bay Area.
    3. Suburbs—California—San Francisco Bay Area.   4. Culture
    conflict—California—San Francisco Bay Area.   5. Minorities—
    California—San Francisco Bay Area—Social conditions.   6. San
    Francisco Bay Area (Calif.)—Race relations.   7. San Francisco Bay
    Area (Calif.)—Ethnic relations.   I. Title.
    HN80.S4R63   1999
    306'.09794'6—dc21   99–21192

British Library Cataloguing in Publication Data is available.

Library of Congress Catalog Card Number: 99–21192
ISBN: 0–275–96406–X

First published in 1999

Praeger Publishers, 88 Post Road West, Westport, CT 06881
An imprint of Greenwood Publishing Group, Inc.
www.praeger.com

Printed in the United States of America

The paper used in this book complies with the
Permanent Paper Standard issued by the National
Information Standards Organization (Z39.48–1984).

10 9 8 7 6 5 4 3 2 1

Copyright Acknowledgments

Every reasonable effort has been made to trace the owners of copyright materials in this book, but
in some instances this has proven impossible. The author and publisher will be glad to receive information leading to more complete acknowledgments in subsequent printings of the book and in the
meantime extend their apologies for any omissions.

This book is dedicated to
the memory of my father, Antonio Rodriguez.

CONTENTS

ILLUSTRATIONS

FIGURES

PHOTOS

ABBREVIATIONS

BANC   Bancroft Library, University of California-Berkeley

CHS   California Historical Society

ITS   Institute of Transportation Studies Library,
University of California-Berkeley

MMCOP   Mason McDuffie Real Estate Company Records,
Bancroft Library, University of California-Berkeley

OHR   Oakland History Room, Oakland Public Library

SFHC   San Francisco History Center,
San Francisco Public Library

ACKNOWLEDGMENTS

I have benefited over the years from the counsel of many friends and colleagues. I especially thank Gunther Barth for his advice, support, and friendship. I am grateful for having colleagues in the History department at the University of Wisconsin-Milwaukee who shared their time and encouraged me to complete this book. Chris Rhomberg generously shared his research on Oakland politics in the 1960s. I am very thankful for funding I received from the University of Wisconsin Institute on Race and Ethnicity. I owe a debt of gratitude to the institute's director, Thomas V. Tonensen, who led a faculty seminar on the culture wars that encouraged me to investigate further the topic. Greg Jay provided a trenchant critique of the introduction. I am also grateful for financial support provided by the University of Wisconsin-Milwaukee Graduate School and the National Endowment for the Humanities. Several librarians helped me locate sources: Jeff Paul at San Jose State University, William Sturm at the Oakland Public Library, and Betty Faffei at the Contra Costa Historical Society. David Ocampo graciously shared his research on the Fiesta de las Rosas riot. Joe Tran of Tran Design and Associates generously scanned several photographs. I thank Donna Schenstrom, director of the UWM Cartographic Services Laboratory, for creating the maps. Heather Staines and Emma Moore, my editors at Praeger, made getting the project into print as painless as possible, and Yoshiko Okano Guy was a godsend during the final production stages. Anita Cathey, Louise Whitaker, and Ernestine Rawls helped solve computer problems. William Velez, Deidre Heitman, Toni Newell, Estrella Sotomayor, and Roger Guy provided much appreciated moral support, friendship, and advice. I could not have completed this book without the love and encouragement of my mother, my sister, and Beth Ayers.

INTRODUCTION

I grew up in San Leandro, a suburb south of Oakland, in the San Francisco Bay Area. San Leandro was named after the rancho established by Joaquín Estudillo in the 1830s. His three daughters married Anglos, two of whom inherited land where they built a hotel in 1855. Though San Leandro was home for numerous Mexicans, Chinese, Japanese, and Filipinos, Anglos dominated town politics.[1]

San Leandro, like many American suburbs, grew rapidly after World War II. It had begun as a streetcar suburb of Oakland, and in the early 1900s, it was a blue-collar suburb with industries located along railroad tracks and the Bay. After the war developers built two- and three-bedroom houses that enticed young families in search of a centrally located East Bay suburb.

By the 1970s, continued rapid growth led some to claim San Leandro's character had changed. In 1973, the city published a history pamphlet in which a local writer praised San Leandro's earliest Hispanic and Anglo inhabitants for their civic mindedness. By comparison, the modern San Leandro resident "no longer resides as a participating citizen, but has become a 'commuter' and is often uninformed and disinterested in the city's historic past." Residents were no longer united, resulting in "the deterioration of many social values and belief systems, leaving many people in a state of 'rootlessness.'"[2] The pamphlet highlighted the town's early Spanish and Anglo settlers with little mention of Asian or Mexican inhabitants, though one article entitled "Forgotten People" examined the vanquished Costano Indians.[3]

During the 1980s, the city's Asian, Latino, and black populations surged to one-third of the city's 72,000 inhabitants. Local officials launched a public relations campaign praising the city's diversity.

"Celebrating diversity means that we recognize that every individual in our community has unique qualities and characteristics that can contribute to the overall richness and vitality of life in San Leandro," read a city brochure published in the mid 1990s. "We acknowledge and take pride in the fact that our community is made up of varied groups of people from all ethnic and cultural backgrounds."[4]

By celebrating multiculturalism, city officials not only acknowledged ethnic diversity, they also responded to the increased density of the city. New condominium and apartment complexes attracted single professionals who commuted from San Leandro to jobs throughout the Bay Area. These new buildings produced urban-like densities, as did the new strip malls that contained new Asian- and Latino-owned shops. Crime and traffic also increased. These changes upset some residents. With urbanization, the city faced an identity crisis. The brochure insisted that San Leandro could keep its "small town charm," while endeavoring to "attract new businesses and a steady stream of home buyers." Yet it repeatedly referred to San Leandro as "the City."

Many American communities, like San Leandro, are currently searching for a unifying identity.[5] The absence of community cohesiveness is often attributed to the growing ethnic diversity of American cities and suburbs. For a variety of reasons, multiculturalism is on the rise and group identities proliferate. While America is becoming more diverse, with immigrants arriving from Asia, Africa, and Latin America, assimilation is no longer the only way that newcomers, particularly non-whites, become integrated into this society. Since the ethnic pride movement of the 1960s, many pressures to assimilate have subsided. Also, immigrants often now arrive as families rather than as single adults. The global economy requires, and modern communication technologies allow, immigrants to remain in constant contact with their homelands. Suburbs now attract immigrants and minorities because new jobs are flourishing in the suburbs.[6]

As more and more Americans assert their separate identities, fears grow about the balkanization of the United States. Opponents of multiculturalism cite the secession movement in Quebec and the wars in Bosnia as resulting from the decline of an overarching civic consciousness. But progressives also criticize multiculturalism for emphasizing ethnic differences that divide the working class and undercut any progressive social movement based on multiracial or multiethnic alliances.[7]

The fight over multiculturalism is considered part of the "culture wars." The term "culture wars" reflects the belief that cultural issues have become more controversial than economic struggles in the United States. Christian conservatives denounce homosexuality and criticize growing acceptance of alternative lifestyles. Gay-rights advocates organize to outlaw sexual preference discrimination. Pro-life groups block entrances to abortion clinics, harass and even murder abortion doctors. Abortion-rights activists defend the clinics and oppose any restriction on the procedure. While Christian groups protest violence and sexual content in the mass media and fight for television and musical record ratings systems, liberals decry increased censorship.[8] Neither side in these struggles will give an inch, and compromise is not possible.

Is America becoming divided into cultural enclaves? And if so, why? Sociologist James Davison Hunter, who coined the term "culture wars," argues that America's recent battles represent a new, highly divisive form of social conflict. The culture wars, he explains, reflect "the struggle to achieve or maintain the power to define reality."[9] Combatants believe that they face an intense struggle to maintain the nation's core values. Arguments over the arts, education, the media, and sexuality gain greater significance as conservatives and liberals compete to shape America's fundamental beliefs.

Hunter argues that there is a fight in America between the "orthodoxy" and the "progressivists." The orthodoxy respects received authority and calls on the nation to abide by traditional values embodied in the Bible and the Constitution, values that the orthodoxy feels have declined along with the American family. The progressive perspective holds that national leaders and institutions have been historically biased and must be reformed to incorporate those Americans traditionally excluded from the nation's political, economic, and cultural mainstream. Both groups increasingly use inflammatory language and the mass media to direct public opinion, discredit adversaries, and disavow compromise.[10]

Several theories explain the origins of the culture wars. Some argue that the culture wars reflect the decline of governmental leadership in the United States since the 1960s. Without strong central leadership the country drifts, and citizens gravitate toward extremist positions that offer simplistic solutions to social problems. The rise of the global economy, moreover, has brought a decline of allegiance to a single state. Workers and companies today cross international borders so frequently that they feel little pressure and have few incentives to adapt to the local culture, creating conflict over cultural and religious values. Another reason cited for the culture wars is the decline of mainline religious authority. Denominational differences are used to express distinct social outlooks. However, with the rise of ecumenicalism, diverse members unite across denominational boundaries. For example, pro-life Catholics unite with pro-life Protestants against pro-choice Catholics and Protestants.[11]

The culture wars also reflect the revolutionary transformation of the American family. With more than 60 percent of all married women with children now working outside the house, the traditional nuclear family, composed of an employed husband and a housewife, is no longer the dominant domestic arrangement. The financial empowerment of working women threatens conservatives who seek a return to a mythical era of "traditional family values," despite declining salaries that mandate that both parents bring home a paycheck.[12]

The shrinking of union membership has meant economic struggles often take a back seat to cultural battles. The decline of industrialism in the United States, and the increasing internationalization of the economy, undercut labor power. Also, union officials tended to overlook the organization of the new service workers, many of whom are women, immigrants, or minorities. Many immigrant workers primarily identify with their national group, thus impeding the development of class consciousness and union loyalty. As a result, just one in six workers today is a union member.[13]

Ethnic and racial identities also became more muddied in the 1970s and 1980s. Despite ongoing assimilation and the elimination of *de jure* discrimination, racial minorities still suffer from political, social, and economic inequalities. During the 1960s, blacks obtained affirmative action provisions that gave government recognition to group rights.[14] The inclusion of Latinos and Asians in affirmative action programs spurred opposition from conservatives and liberals, whites, and some minorities to any preferences given based on race or gender. Racial segregation in housing continues to divide America, yet a growing number of middle-class minorities moved out of the ghettos and barrios and some led the fight against affirmative action.[15]

Although increased immigration, the decline of assimilation, the breaking apart of religious affiliations, and the transformed American family all contributed to the culture wars, to understand them fully we need to move beyond vague notions about the rise of identity politics. We need to look at urban and suburban change. This study analyzes four conflicts in the San Francisco Bay Area from the 1960s to the 1990s. These struggles, and many others in the culture wars, were touched off by the rise of a new American metropolitan region composed of numerous interconnected cities and suburbs. With the advent of freeways and rapid transit, modern metropolitan mobility brought the convergence of city and suburb and the erasure of local community identities and traditions. As city and suburb merged, local leaders searched for a unifying community identity. Local reaction to urban-suburban change took the form of criticism of new projects that brought outsiders while obscuring local history and culture. This stimulated sharp conflicts between residents and leaders. The rise of commuting and the loss of a sense of community led San Leandro officials to turn to local history to unify their town in the 1970s. In the 1980s their search for a unified community identity continued, leading officials to promote multiculturalism. Metropolitan growth during the 1970s had enmeshed San Leandro within a larger region, which threatened its autonomy and diminished its sense of community. But determining a new community identity often stimulated new conflicts as the chapters that follow will show.

THE MULTICENTERED METROPOLIS

Jean Gottmann in 1961 argued that the northeastern seaboard cities from Boston to Washington D.C. were converging into a solidly urbanized mega-city.[16] Gottmann was one of the first scholars to realize that twentieth-century urban America was undergoing a spatial revolution. Since World War II, urban growth had occurred most rapidly on the fringes of the metropolitan region. By the 1960s more Americans lived in suburbs than in cities, and by the 1970s more office space existed in the suburbs than in the cities. Metropolitan areas became city-regions composed of multiple interconnected cities, forming what Pierce Lewis called the "galactic" city.[17] Others named it the city-region, the multicentered, multinucleated or polycentric metropolis, the postsuburban city, the technoburb, exurbia, or exopolis.[18]

The multicentered metropolis is characterized by growth occurring fastest on the edges of the region around several suburban "edge cities" of equal importance. These former suburbs now boast growing downtowns where office buildings lure thousands of commuters. No longer are suburbs simply bedroom communities while cities control jobs, industry, and entertainment. Many parts of the urban economy have decentralized. Americans now often travel each day from a house in one suburb to a job in another, and avoid the city all together.[19] The multicentered metropolis sprawls along highways over a much larger space than the pre-World War II city.[20]

How did this new multicentered metropolitan form occur and what are its social consequences? Some argue it was due to transportation changes, particularly the rise of the automobile and freeways. Beginning in the early 1800s, ferries, then horsecar, railroad, and streetcar lines linked city and suburb in the classic "star" or hub and spoke pattern, connecting suburbanites with central city offices and stores. This regional pattern situated development along the space beside the transit lines, greatly limiting the overall size of the metropolitan area. It also limited the ability of suburbs to compete with the central city for regional economic development because the suburbs were connected to the city and had few links to other suburbs. But the early transit network provided the suburbs with their chief attraction, their slow growth, stable neighborhoods, and rural character.[21]

The construction of new highways and freeways after World War II made it possible for suburbs to compete economically with cities. The new highways and freeways spurred the trucking industry, which competed with railroads for the shipment of products. Taking advantage of the new connections, suburban leaders enticed businesses to the hinterland with lower taxes, fewer regulations, cheaper land, and open space. The Federal Housing Administration insured long-term, low-interest mortgages which stimulated the massive suburban movement of middle-class home buyers.[22]

Many post-war changes in business technology also stimulated the urbanization of the suburbs. In the early 1900s, electric power eliminated the requirement of locating a business near coal deposits or railroad lines. After the war, industrial automation required sprawling one-story plants, which made urban location expensive and suburban locations necessary.[23] By the 1970s, the advent of computer technology encouraged high-tech companies to locate near a research university, such as Stanford University in the Santa Clara Valley, where employers found young engineers who brought talent and connections to defense-related government research funding.[24] Computers and satellites allowed instant communication across the city, the country, and around the world, allowing company offices to be located in the most attractive and cost-effective locations.

The availability of natural resources on the periphery also led to urban growth in the suburbs. In Los Angeles, the presence of oil deposits led to the construction of boom towns where workers labored in oil fields, and later in aircraft industries like Northrop and Lockheed, also located in the hinterland to take advantage of open space, which housed expanded production facilities made necessary by government orders for many new aircraft.[25]

Ongoing racial prejudice and fear of declining home values spurred the flight by whites from the cities to the suburbs. As middle-class whites moved to the suburbs the cities became dominated by poor minorities. Companies left to avoid the black workforce, the labor unions that dominated urban employment, increasing taxes, and regulations. The urban riots of the 1960s made business owners and middle-class residents leery of investing in the city. Prejudice and poverty produced poor urban schools and many parents desired to get their children into suburban classrooms.

Business owners who moved to the suburbs for personal or family reasons simply took their enterprises along. They wanted to live near their offices and shorten their personal commutes. This preference for the suburbs extended to employees, and so employers lured highly sought after computer scientists by setting up research facilities in attractive suburban areas.[26] Employers also moved to employ non-unionized housewives. Business executives who made frequent air flights established offices near suburban airports to save time and resources.

Finally, the multicentered metropolis resulted from the shift of the U.S. economy from manufacturing and industry to services, information collection, and entertainment. The processing of information, by government, financial institutions, advertising and entertainment companies, and law firms, has expanded to more than 50 percent of the total U.S. economy since World War II. Increasingly, data processing is done in suburban offices over computer networks and telephone lines.[27]

While the rise of the multicentered metropolis has received analysis, there has been little discussion of its cultural consequences. Most analysis of the impact of decentralized growth focuses on the dire effect of suburbs on the central city. Though suburban growth had a profound impact on the city, the multicentered metropolis had other significant consequences. Notably, decentralized urbanization mandated increased regional mobility, giving consumers greater choice in where to live, work, and play. Americans now living within a metropolitan region, Robert Fishman notes, "create their own city from the multitude of destinations that are within suitable driving distance."[28] Each day, Americans drive from house, to job, to mall, and to supermarket, each, perhaps, located in a different city. Only the road links the various destinations within this fragmented region, and a town loses its distinctive character. "People concern themselves less with places and more with functions, and place becomes simply the location of an institution providing a functional fulfillment," notes David Brodsly. "Redondo has a nice beach, Venice a good movie theater, and Long Beach a good Mexican restaurant, but all lose their identity as coherent environments."[29] The urbanized region encourages anonymity and individualism. We feel like outsiders since we so frequently venture beyond our own neighborhoods and communities. Our own communities cater to outsiders who now are an increasingly important element of all local transactions within the multicentered metropolis. Communities are transient, forming quickly, and residents come and go as new communities rise further out in the hinterland.[30]

The rise of the multicentered metropolis also transformed the way Americans think about the relationship between city and suburb. Prior to the twentieth century, most Americans believed city and suburb played separate but equally valuable roles within the metropolitan region. City and suburb were complimentary and not conflictive environments. The city dominated the regional economy and was the fount of culture, education, business, and industry. The suburb was less populous and more economically homogeneous than the city, and contained much less traffic and noise. The suburb provided a calm domestic environment and a reprieve from the hectic pace of the city. From the city came new ideas, inventions, and consumer products. The city produced the wealth necessary for residents to live comfortably in the suburb. Immigrants first settled in the urban tenements, became acculturated, found better jobs, and then moved out to the suburb. As they left the city for the suburb, newly arriving immigrants and migrants took their place in the city.[31] Elites often owned both an urban residence and a suburban retreat.[32]

Streetcar lines ended at suburban amusement parks which provided recreation and a chance for city dwellers to experience nature. From the suburban periphery came the natural resources necessary for urban industries. The fact that some American suburbs took the name of cities, such as West Chicago and East St. Louis, indicated their mutual dependence and respect.[33]

After World War II, the urban-suburban relationship changed dramatically. Whereas in the nineteenth century Americans viewed the city and suburb as complimentary, by the 1960s they viewed them as antagonistic. As freeways, telephones, faxes, and computers greatly weakened the central city's hold on business, more suburbanites began working in other suburbs rather than in the city.[34] City and suburb now competed for workers and businesses.

After World War II, Americans began comparing city and suburb in negative ways. Scholars and urban officials began blaming city problems on the movement to the suburbs of jobs and middle-class residents. These experts concluded that "suburbs exploit cities and cause their decline."[35] Besides sapping the city of its economic potency, city supporters argued that the suburbs, by excluding minorities from newer housing, trapped the poor in urban neighborhoods.[36] These urban experts also lambasted suburbs for their "ticky tack" houses, conformist culture, racial and class homogeneity, absence of cultural amenities, and any sense of social responsibility toward the less fortunate. Lewis Mumford, a city advocate, lambasted modern suburbia for "a multitude of houses lined up inflexibly, at uniform distances, on uniform roads, in a treeless communal waste."[37]

Conversely, suburbanites attacked urban corruption, poor schools, crumbling streets, rusting transit, mounting crime, desolate environment, and lack of community. Suburban residents increasingly avoided any trip to the city or, when forced to go, took the new freeways that led directly to parking garages connected by skywalks to symphony halls, museums, hospitals, and office buildings. For most suburbanites, their only image of the city came from the crime scene reports on the nightly news.[38] Americans increasingly viewed the suburb as the "anti-city" rather than a space that contained both urban and rural elements in a pleasing balance.

The estrangement of city and suburb, however, did not preclude leaders from sharing planning ideas. As businesses lured commuters into the suburbs, officials adapted urban design elements to the suburban environment. This produced what some call the urbanization of the suburbs.[39] Suburbs now boast downtowns with office buildings, shopping districts, and central plazas creating a sense of urban excitement and population density.[40] As new businesses attract younger singles and non-whites, suburban communities seek to diversify their shopping and entertainment offerings to appeal to the newcomers. Suburban leaders support the construction of performing arts centers and museums, often financed by taxing corporate developers.[41] Urban densities are approached in the suburbs as developers facing restrictions on sprawl and increased utility costs build new projects on vacant land available within older suburbs.[42]

While the urbanization of the suburbs is often discussed, the converse trend, the suburbanization of the city, has received less attention. American cities, geographer Joseph S. Wood argues, are becoming suburbanized, as indicated by the construction of downtown shopping malls, low-density housing, parks and open spaces, parking garages, freeways, and the out-migration of heavy manufacturing. Moreover, the new downtown exemplifies a "corporate middle-class definition of space and place" most concerned with public safety, hygiene, and order.[43] As cities lost population, their densities have approached those in the suburbs.[44]

By bringing suburbia to the city, urban leaders attempted to maintain the city's middle-class population while attracting suburbanites into entertainment, shopping, housing, and employment areas. They built motels, drive-through restaurants and banks, and widened boulevards to accommodate the suburban motorist.[45] Cities hired more police officers to patrol downtown and added skywalks that isolated shoppers above threatening streets.[46] Other scholars view urban gentrification and gated communities as attempts to suburbanize the city.[47] The quest by urban residents to use property taxes to pay for private school tuition amounts to seceding from the urban public school system without having to leave for the suburbs.[48]

While cities and suburbs may have converged in physical terms, they have not merged within the minds of most Americans. Sociologist David Hummon concluded that Americans today hold conflicting impressions of cities, suburbs, and small towns. Hummon asked urban and suburban residents what they felt about their communities. Urban informants described cities as diverse, vibrant, modern, stimulating, and culturally exciting. In contrast, they viewed suburbs as tradition-bound, homogeneous, slow-paced, and provincial. His suburban respondents, on the other hand, viewed cities as overwhelming, anonymous, impersonal, bureaucratic, dangerous, and hostile. But they characterized suburbs as friendly, family and community oriented, and wholesome. Thus, Americans understand city and suburb as essentially different, despite ongoing social, cultural, and economic convergence.[49]

Because Americans continue to identify city and suburb as contrasting environments, the suburbanization of cities and the urbanization of suburbs produces clashes between residents over how to define their community and which values to maintain in the face of increased regional interaction. When city people fought freeways or chain stores, they expressed opposition to the suburbanization of the city and the perceived loss of urban cosmopolitanism. When suburbanites rallied against new high-rises, or modern art, they fought the intrusion of an unwanted urban culture, which they felt denigrated suburban values.

Urbanites have come to see their city's suburbanization as a threat to the city's true identity as a cosmopolitan community. A recent letter writer to the *New York Times* summed up this position when she criticized plans for "suburban-style mega-structures" in New York City. "I am a New Yorker because I hate the rest of America," wrote Julie Scelfo. "I hate driving one mile and passing four strip malls. New York as I knew it is dying, its landscape is already denigrated by the Gap signs and the Starbucks on every corner."[50] Scelfo defended New York's cosmopolitan urban culture against the suburban culture ("strip malls") that she feels is homogenizing the city's landscape.

Yet many suburbanites would similarly reject the proliferation of Gap stores and Starbucks in their communities. But they would protest them as part of an unwanted outside urban culture that has diminished their suburban, family-centered community. The struggles over community identities discussed in *City Against Suburb* emerged from the convergence of city and suburb that followed the construction of the regional transportation networks.

By the mid-twentieth century, many Americans had concluded that cities and suburbs represented completely different, and conflicting, cultural values. They began talking about an "urban culture" and a "suburban culture" as representing distinct outlooks and ways of life. Whereas cities ideally stood for "an openness to unassimilated otherness," the suburbs epitomized the desire for a cohesive environment where communities and families flourished.[51] The convergence of city and suburb, therefore, produced culture wars.

THE SAN FRANCISCO BAY AREA

The San Francisco Bay Area is a particularly appropriate setting for this study linking the culture wars to the urban and suburban effects of regional mobility. From its earliest days in the nineteenth century, the geography of the Bay Area mandated a dispersed pattern of settlement (Figure 1). Isolated at the end of a peninsula, San Francisco soon faced competing towns, like little Benicia on the mainland side, which early observers anticipated would one day surpass San Francisco. They were right. San Jose is now the largest city in the Bay Area. While San Francisco grew up around the shipping industry, Oakland came of age during the streetcar era, and San Jose matured during the automobile period and sprawls throughout the Santa Clara Valley. Geography limited San Francisco's dominance over regional transportation.

Figure 1.
San Francisco Bay Area

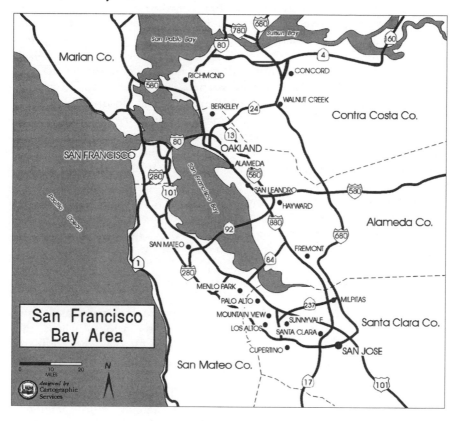

Nevertheless, San Francisco, Oakland, and San Jose all extended transit links throughout the Bay Area, which produced, by the mid-twentieth century, an efficient, multifaceted transportation network.[52]   The existence of freeways and the Bay Area Rapid Transit (BART) by the 1970s led local leaders to encourage residents from throughout the region to visit, work, and live in their cities or suburbs.   But some residents criticized these efforts by their leaders to attract outsiders from throughout the region, and they protested transit connections that they felt undermined local culture and traditions.

The Bay Area's geography channeled urban development along distinct paths. San Francisco may be the most European-like city in the United States, but beginning in the 1840s towns sprouted up along the Bayshore.[53] The mountains and the Bay forced the construction of railroad and streetcar lines, highways, and BART along nearly the same

routes.   Each new transportation technology transformed settlements
built around a preceding transit system.   For example, Oakland began as
a ferry suburb of San Francisco, but the streetcars in the early 1900s
helped transform it into a city.   Berkeley began as a ferry-streetcar suburb
of San Francisco and Oakland and evolved into a city during the
automobile era.[54]

Besides geography, urban rivalry played a fundamental role in shaping
Bay Area urbanism.   The geographical barriers intensified urban competition in the region.   San Francisco, Oakland, and San Jose built separate
railroad terminals, streetcar lines, airports, and downtowns, tapped
different sources for drinking water, and vied for major sports teams.
Geography limited San Francisco's regional influence and encouraged
Oakland and San Jose to compete for regional status rather than simply
accept San Francisco's leadership.

Bay Area urban rivalries led to calls for regional planning boards.   The
first attempt at regional cooperation, the Regional Plan Association
(RPA), was founded in San Francisco in the 1920s to deal with regional
issues concerning harbors, highways, rapid transit, zoning, parks, and
water pollution.   The RPA never drew support from Oakland leaders who
viewed with suspicion its San Francisco origins.[55]   Toward the end of
World War II, San Francisco and Oakland business leaders formed the
Bay Area Council (BAC), which sought to improve regional transit and
harbor facilities.   Government officials in the early 1960s formed the
Association of Bay Area Governments (ABAG).   Despite these efforts,
regional planning largely failed.   Thus, urban rivalry spurred regional
planning proposals and also undercut those same efforts as Bay Area city
leaders fought to maintain their power over local development.

Though these regional government efforts largely failed, regional
issues were always an important part of the Bay Area's political culture.
All transportation projects that linked cities around the Bay, including
ferries, railroads, streetcars, bridges, and highways, made apparent both
the need for regional cooperation and the existence of jealousies and fears
among urban leaders.   For example, during the construction of the Bay
Bridge in the 1930s, San Francisco and Oakland leaders waxed eloquent
about how the giant span would bring a future of regional cooperation.
Yet upon completion, they could not even agree on which side of the
bridge to stage the opening day ceremonies, and so state and local
officials had to make speeches, pose for photographs, and cut a steel chain
at either end of the span.[56]

The construction of new freeways in the 1950s and BART in the 1960s
also mandated serious discussions about regional cooperation.   State
officials insisted that freeways serve regional interests and not those of a
particular city, while urban leaders feared that the freeways would
undercut local aspirations if state engineers failed to respond to their

design concerns. Bay Area residents and officials celebrated BART as a transit system that would finally tie the metropolis together and encourage greater cooperation. But they feared that BART and its regional board would make design decisions that benefited their rivals and hurt local development. In the end, these projects, by leading to the suburbanization of the city and the urbanization of the suburbs, drew criticism from residents and leaders for having a negative impact on community traditions and identities.

Part one analyzes the suburbanization of the city in the Bay Area. Chapter one traces the opposition of middle-class San Franciscans to the construction of freeways through their city from the mid 1950s to the mid 1960s. While city planners had long insisted that a better highway system was necessary if San Francisco was to remain the center of the Bay Area metropolis, opponents believed that the freeways would destroy its urban culture, transforming San Francisco into one of several indistinguishable suburbs around the Bay. The fact the freeways threatened two particularly important urban symbols, the Ferry building and Golden Gate Park, intensified the conflict. The two structures embodied San Francisco's cosmopolitan urban culture. The threat to these urban symbols infuriated freeway opponents who viewed the expressways and the automobile as bringing suburban culture to the city.

In chapter two, the analysis of the struggle over the value of regional mobility shifts to Oakland. In the mid 1960s, proponents of BART clashed with working-class and minority residents in the West Oakland neighborhood. BART officials touted regional mobility as beneficial to the working-class and minority communities. Minority leaders, however, argued that BART imposed a suburban-based, individualistic culture on West Oakland, undermining their urban neighborhood where a culture of cooperative communalism thrived. West Oakland leaders proposed that BART implement an affirmative action program, arguing that BART had a responsibility to the community since it displaced local residents and suburbanized jobs.

Part two analyzes the local struggles over the urbanization of the suburbs. Chapter three focuses on San Jose, which in the 1950s critics called a giant sprawling suburb. Despite its overall prosperity, the city's downtown declined as consumers patronized new shopping malls established on the city's fringe. Hoping to reverse that trend and give downtown an urban identity, San Jose merchants launched a public relations campaign celebrating the city's origins as a Spanish pueblo. They gained the support of middle-class Mexican Americans who helped sponsor a pageant called "La Fiesta de las Rosas" in 1969. Younger Chicano activists, however, criticized the use of Chicano history to stimulate downtown business. They demanded that the city concentrate on meeting the needs of local residents, particularly the poor living near the downtown in the city's eastside barrios. They rejected the public relations effort to lure outsiders into the downtown, and they insisted that the fiesta misrepresented local history by ignoring the history of Spanish and Anglo appropriation of Native American and Mexican land.

The urbanization of the suburb of Concord in the 1980s is the subject of chapter four. Concord began as a rural town, then evolved into a suburb in the 1950s and 1960s. In the 1980s, corporate banks built several high-rises in Concord's downtown. Local leaders wanted to further Concord's evolution from a bedroom community into an exciting city by investing in public art to entice commuters who worked in the bank offices and other outsiders into downtown shops and restaurants. They used taxes on new development to finance a large sculpture called "Spirit Poles." Located along Concord Avenue, the large, abstract sculpture offended the aesthetic sensibilities of many residents. Residents lambasted the modern art piece as antithetical to the community's family-centered, suburban identity, and insisted that the sculpture was appropriate for big cities like San Francisco and New York, but not Concord. Yet Concord was diversifying. It was in fact no longer simply a suburb. The conflict forced Concord residents to discuss its evolving community identity.

In these four struggles, regional mobility brought the convergence of city and suburb, which motivated action by residents seeking to maintain community traditions in the face of rapid change. At times, local activists fought growth, but slowing growth was not their chief motivation. Rather, residents in San Francisco, Oakland, San Jose, and Concord reacted against new freeways, rapid transit, and downtown redevelopment that they saw as evidence of a regional culture that would replace local traditions. As freeways and BART suburbanized cities and urbanized suburbs, local residents acted to defend their city's or suburb's original cultural identity.[57] Thus, this study focuses on one of the most contentious and often overlooked battles of the culture wars, the ongoing cultural struggle between cities and suburbs in America's metropolitan regions.

NOTES

1. Harry E. Shaffer, *A Garden Grows in Eden: The Centennial Story of San Leandro* (San Leandro, 1972).

2. *Saga of San Leandro*, Local History Studies, vol. 13, California History Center (Cupertino, 1973), ii.

3. Ibid.

4. Brochure in possession of author.

5. Perhaps the most studied community is Monterey Park in southern California.

See Timothy P. Fong, *The First Suburban Chinatown: The Remaking of Monterey Park California* (Philadelphia, 1994); John Horton, *The Politics of Diversity: Immigration, Resistance, and Change in Monterey Park, California* (Philadelphia, 1995); Leland Seito, *Race and Politics: Asian Americans, Latinos and Whites in a Los Angeles Suburb* (Urbana, 1998).

6.   See for example Joseph Wood, "Vietnamese Place Making in Northern Virginia," *Geographical Review* 87, no. 1 (January 1997): 58–72.

7.   See Todd Gitlin, *The Twilight of Common Dreams: Why America is Wracked by Culture Wars* (New York, 1995); Nancy Fraser, *Justice Interruptus: Critical Reflections on the "Postsocialist" Condition* (New York, 1997), 11–33.

8.   Tricia Rose, *Black Noise: Rap Music and Black Culture in Contemporary America* (Hanover, 1994).

9.   James Davison Hunter, *Culture Wars: The Struggle to Define America* (New York, 1991).

10.   Hunter, *Culture Wars*, ch. 5.

11.   Hunter, *Culture Wars*, 97–104; See also Arthur M. Schlesinger, Jr., *The Disuniting of America: Reflections of a Multicultural Society* (New York, 1991); Allan Bloom, *The Closing of the American Mind* (New York, 1987); Richard Bernstein, *Dictatorship of Virtue: Multiculturalism and the Battle for America's Future* (New York, 1994); John C. Green et al., *Religion and the Culture Wars: Dispatches from the Front* (New York, 1996).

12.   See Arlene Skolnick, *Embattled Paradise: The American Family in an Age of Uncertainty* (New York, 1991); Stephanie Coontz, *The Way We Really Are: Coming to Terms with America's Changing Families* (New York, 1997); Pamela Johnston Conover, *Feminism and the New Right: Conflict Over the American Family* (New York, 1983).

13.   Gitlin, *Twilight of Common Dreams*, 226.

14.   The irony today is that liberals support affirmative action, a policy that big business initially proposed to co-opt radical social movements of the 1960s. See John David Skrentny, *The Ironies of Affirmative Action* (Chicago, 1996).

15.   On black conservatives, see Robin D. G. Kelley, *Yo' Mama's Disfunktional!: Fighting the Culture Wars in Urban America* (Boston, 1997), 89. See also Linda Chavez, *Out of the Barrio: Toward a New Politics of Hispanic Assimilation* (New York, 1991); Lydia Chavez, *The Color Bind: California's Battle to End Affirmative Action* (Berkeley, 1998).

16.   Jean Gottmann, *Megalopolis: The Urbanized Northeastern Seaboard of the United States* (New York, 1961).

17.   The term "city-region" is employed by Robert Geddes, "Metropolis Unbound: The Sprawling American City and the Search for Alternatives," *The American Prospect* 35 (November-December 1997): 40–46; Pierce F. Lewis, "The Galactic Metropolis," *Annals of the American Academy of Political and Social Science* 422 (November 1975): 23–50.

18.   See Peter O. Muller, *Contemporary Suburban America* (Englewood Cliffs, 1981); and Peter O. Muller, *The Outer City: Geographical Consequences of the Urbanization of the Suburbs* (Washington D.C., 1976); Robert Fishman, *Bourgeois Utopias: The Rise and Fall of Suburbia* (New York, 1987).

19.   See Robert Fishman, "America's New City: Megalopolis Unbound," *Wilson Quarterly* (Winter 1990): 25.

20.   Fishman, "America's New City," 28. See also Edward Soja, "Inside Exopolis: Scenes from Orange County," in Michael Sorkin, ed., *Variations on a Theme Park: The New American City and the End of Public Space* (New York, 1992).

21.   See Kenneth T. Jackson, *Crabgrass Frontier: The Suburbanization of the United States* (New York, 1985); John R. Stilgoe, *Borderland: Origins of the American Suburb: 1820-1939* (New Haven, 1988).

22.   Jackson, *Crabgrass Frontier*, 204. On housing in the 1930s, see Gail Radford, *Modern Housing for America: Policy Struggles in the New Deal Era* (Chicago, 1996).

23. Thomas J. Sugrue, *Origins of the Urban Crisis: Race and Inequality in Postwar Detroit* (Princeton, 1996), 130–135.

24. See Everett M. Rogers and Judith K. Larsen, *Silicon Valley Fever: Growth of High-Technology Culture* (New York, 1986), 39.

25. See Greg Hise, "Home Building and Industrial Decentralization in Los Angeles: The Roots of the Postwar Urban Region," *Journal of Urban History* 19, no. 2 (February 1993): 95–125; and Fred W. Viehe, "Black Gold Suburbs: The Influence of the Extractive Industry on the Suburbanizaton of Los Angeles, 1890-1930," *Journal of Urban History* 8, no. 1 (1981): 3–26.

26. M. Gottdiener and George Kephart, "The Multinucleated Metropolitan Region: A Comparative Analysis," in Rob Kling, Spencer Olin, and Mark Poster, eds., *Postsuburban California: The Transformation of Orange County Since World War II* (Berkeley, 1991), 35–39.

27. David Lyon, *The Information Society: Issues and Illusions* (New York, 1988).

28. Fishman, *Bourgeois Utopias*, 185.

29. David Brodsly, *L.A. Freeway: An Appreciative Essay* (Berkeley, 1981), 33.

30. See John P. Hewitt, *Dilemmas of the American Self* (Philadelphia, 1989), 92; Claude S. Fischer, "Ambivalent Communities: How Americans Understand Their Localities," in Alan Wolfe, ed., *America at Century's End* (Berkeley, 1991), 79–90.

31. Clay McShane, *Down the Asphalt Path: The Automobile and the American City* (New York, 1994), 226.

32. Lewis Mumford, *The City in History: Its Origins, Its Transformations, and Its Prospects* (New York, 1961), 483.

33. See Jackson, *Crabgrass Frontier*, 272; Stilgoe, Borderland, 32.

34. See Joel Garreau, *Edge City: Life on the New Frontier* (New York, 1991).

35. See the critique of this conclusion by Brett W. Hawkins and Roberta Derlin, "Do Suburbs Harm Cities? A Review of the Evidence," *Research and Opinion* 11, no. 3 (June 1997): 1. See also Brett W. Hawkins and Stephen L. Percy, "On Anti-Suburban Orthodoxy," *Social Sciences Quarterly* 72, no. 3 (September 1991): 478–488.

36. Robert A. Beauregard, *Voices of Decline: The Postwar Fate of U.S. Cities* (Cambridge, 1993), 191–193.

37. See Mumford, *City in History*, 486.

38. Critics of the suburbs were definitely in the minority. Most Americans found in the suburbs the opportunity to buy a bigger and newer house and access to a better school system.

39. See David L. Birch, "From Suburb to Urban Place," *Annals of the American Academy of Political and Social Science* 422 (November 1975): 25–35.

40. See Joseph S. Wood, "Suburbanization of City Center," *Geographical Review* 78, no. 3 (July 1988): 325–329.

41. See Bruce Weber, "Cities are Fostering the Arts as a Way to Save Downtown," *New York Times*, November 18, 1997. For the view that suburbs are not becoming cities see William Sharpe and Leonard Wallock, "Bold New City or Built-up 'Burb'? Redefining Contemporary Suburbia," *American Quarterly* 46 (March 1994): 1–30.

42. On housing infill, see Community Design Center Program, *Residential Infill: Increasing the Opportunity for Affordable Housing* (Berkeley, 1983); Real Estate Research Corporation, *Infill Development Strategies* (Washington D.C., 1982).

43. Wood, "Suburbanization of City Center," 325–329.

44. See Harold Mayer, "The Pull of Land and Space," in Jean Gottmann and Robert A. Harper, *Metropolis on the Move: Geographers Look at Urban Sprawl* (New York, 1967), 31.

45. See John Brinckerhoff Jackson, *A Sense of Place, A Sense of Time* (New Haven, 1994), 183.

46. On skywalks, see Jack Byers, "Privatization of Downtown Public Space," *Journal*

of Planning Education and Research 17 (Spring 1998), 189–205.

47. See Neil Smith, "New City, New Frontier: The Lower East Side as Wild, Wild West," in Sorkin, ed., *Variations on a Theme Park*; and R. Timothy Sieber, "Public Access on the Urban Waterfront: A Question of Vision," in Robert Rotenberg and Gary McDonogh, eds., *The Cultural Meaning of Urban Space* (Westport, 1993).

48. Evan McKenzie, *Privatopia: Homeowner Associations and the Rise of Residential Private Government* (New Haven, 1994), 188.

49. David M. Hummon, *Commonplaces: Community Ideology and Identity in American Culture* (Albany, 1990), 170–172; Constance Perin, *Belonging in America: Reading Between the Lines* (Madison, 1988), 97.

50. *New York Times*, October 22, 1996.

51. See Peter Hall, "The Urban Culture and the Suburban Culture," in Richard Eells and Clarence Walton, eds., *Man in the City of the Future: A Symposium of Urban Philosophers* (New York, 1968); Iris Marion Young, *Justice and the Politics of Difference* (Princeton, 1990), 227.

52. James E. Vance, Jr., *Geography and Urban Evolution in the San Francisco Bay Area* (Berkeley, 1964), 84–86.

53. Vance, *Geography and Urban Evolution*, 34.

54. On Oakland, see Beth Bagwell, *Oakland: The Story of a City* (Oakland, 1982). On Berkeley, see Phil McArdle, ed., *Exactly Opposite the Golden Gate: Essays on Berkeley's History* (Berkeley, 1986).

55. See Mel Scott, *The San Francisco Bay Area: A Metropolis in Perspective*, 2d ed. (Berkeley, 1985), 188–201.

56. See *San Francisco Chronicle*, November 12, 1936.

57. Robert Fisher, "Organizing in the Modern Metropolis: Considering New Social Movement Theory," *Journal of Urban History* 18, no. 2 (February 1992): 225.

PART ONE

———◆———

CITY INTO SUBURB

1

THE FREEWAY REVOLT
IN SAN FRANCISCO

The culture wars ostensibly have little to do with the automobile. Yet in a 1997 article in *Commentary*, James Q. Wilson assails car critics who complain about the proliferation of automobiles. Those with autophobia blame the car for everything wrong about America. They complain that cars lead to ugly suburban architecture, snarled commutes, air pollution, and energy and land depletion. Government subsidies for highways cause the decline of mass transit and decimate cities. Freeways displace urban residents and speed decentralization. Liberals argue that as businesses move to the suburbs, jobs proliferate beyond the reach of low-income Americans who do not own automobiles. Thus, spending tax revenues on freeways rather than mass transit directly harms the poor.[1]

In his article, Wilson raises the specter of a growing movement to do away with cars. While he exaggerates the threat, some do see cars as their worst enemy. In a recent article, environmental scholars Julia Meaton and David Morrice support restrictions on automobiles and argue that although a total ban on the private car is "justifiable," it is currently inadvisable. They propose instead immediate restrictions on automobile use in preparation for a total ban.[2]

Wilson sees these attacks on the automobile as evidence of hostility among some Americans toward suburbs. Both liberals and conservatives blame the automobile for sprawling suburbs. Liberals tend to focus on the suburban threat to cities, the destruction of open space, the depletion of natural resources, segregation, and air and water pollution. Conservatives, meanwhile, indict the suburbs for leading to heightened material-ism, pollution, crass architecture, long commutes, and lack of civic involvement.[3]

Critics often use the word "culture" when talking about the

automobile's impact.   Historian James J. Flink titled his book on the history of the automobile industry *The Car Culture*.[4]   One reader wrote to *Commentary* that "to criticize the car culture is to question the car's dominance over our lives and landscape and the excess of the automobile age."[5]   Similarly, the historian Kenneth T. Jackson used the phrase "drive-in culture" in his study of American suburbanization.[6]   Thus, many Americans believe that the car has had a cultural impact well beyond that of many other modern technologies.   The debate over the car's cultural effects dates to its mass production in the early 1900s.   Clay McShane, also an historian, notes that in the early 1900s, the automobile "served as a battlefield in the wars over gender roles," as men and women argued about whether women should drive, and the impact of women drivers on the family and on femininity.[7]

Many see the car as aiding in the suburbanization of jobs and people, which harms the city.   However, one early historian of the car, John Rae, argued that the automobile did just the opposite.   The automobile "culturally urbanized" rural communities by making urban consumer goods more accessible to country folks.[8]   Rather than seeing the car as bringing urban culture to the suburbs, Wilson argues that the car allows suburbanites to separate from the city.   Without the car, he insists, Americans would be forced to reside within walking or biking distance from a train station.   For Wilson, such compact settlement would be a nightmare, producing "life as it is now lived in Manhattan."   Wilson's disdain for big cities leads him to laud the suburbs for nurturing a sense of community and providing for a better family life.   The suburbs, he insists, are not "inhospitable, rootless, isolated, untraditional or lacking in daily interactions," as their detractors suggest.   Rather, for Wilson, suburban "life is organized around the family, for which there is a lot of time."[9]   Thus, his urban nightmare and his suburban dream lay at the foundation of his defense of the automobile, and fear that some are conspiring to revoke his license.

The debate over the car is part of the culture wars, though not usually recognized as such.   Like Wilson, defenders of suburbia support the automobile for liberating Americans from urban life, and for making possible small towns that nurture families.   But those who favor urban culture see the car as a threat to the social tolerance that prevails in multicultural cities, and associate the decline of American cities and urban culture with increased racial conflict and class animosity.[10]   Like the culture war debates over history, religion, sexuality, and the family, the car wars create sharply divided factions.   Throughout the country, Americans are involved in the car wars, arguing about traffic control, pollution, mass transit, gas taxes, strip malls, landscaping, and freeway construction or removal.   While the car wars debates began in the 1920s, they remain a vital, but often overlooked part of American politics.

THE NEIGHBORHOOD BATTLE

During the 1950s and 1960s, San Franciscans clashed over the construction of freeways in their city. Up until the 1950s, shortage of funding largely limited freeways to rural areas. But the 1956 Interstate Highway Act mandated that fuel tax revenues be spent for highway construction. The federal government began paying 90 percent of the cost of freeways, making urban arteries possible. State and federal engineers supported freeways as did construction unions, the gasoline, automobile, and trucking industries, and the military, which argued Americans could use expressways to flee cities in the event of a nuclear strike. [11]

But urban freeways sometimes forced homeowners to abandon their houses. As a result, protests occurred throughout the country. In the 1950s and 1960s, New York public works head Robert Moses built freeways that displaced many, as did officials in Boston and Chicago. In New Orleans, preservationists fought to exclude freeways from a historic district. In Los Angeles, Chicanos protested freeway construction through their barrios. In many cases such protests failed. [12]

Since the nineteenth century, leaders of San Francisco and cross-bay rival Oakland, continuously competed for economic growth by building new connections to distant parts of the Bay Area. When Oakland was chosen as the Bay Area transcontinental terminal in 1869, San Francisco leaders realized that a bridge was needed across the Bay to bring the trains directly to their city. Though a bridge proved too expensive, they did finance a railroad line built down the peninsula to San Jose, which eventually brought transcontinental trains to their city. [13] This competition between Oakland and San Francisco, joined later by San Jose, resulted in the creation of an extensive transit system linking all parts of the Bay Area.

Urban competition continued to motivate transit improvements in the 1920s when San Francisco leaders grew concerned that increasing congestion would lead more businesses and residents to relocate to the East Bay. Authors of a 1927 study devoted a whole chapter to the need for new highways to eliminate downtown traffic. The chapter entitled "Street Congestion Causes Premature Decentralization" noted that residents living along the peninsula would avoid San Francisco's downtown stores unless new viaducts and parkway boulevards were constructed. [14] The Key System streetcar network, which speeded East Bay suburban residents into downtown San Francisco, also alarmed city leaders who feared that many residents would take up residence across the Bay if the city's transportation system was not improved. This fear led them to call for a subway system down Market Street. [15]

By the 1950s, the San Francisco Chamber of Commerce, the mayor, city supervisors, and city planners saw freeways as necessary to maintain San Francisco's dominant position as the Bay Area's central metropolis.

Beginning in the 1930s, Oakland had aggressively pushed for more state highway money to build connections to its port throughout the East Bay, including the Caldecott Tunnel and the Posey Tube, and East Shore highways. In the 1940s, Oakland leaders complained that San Francisco received the lion's share of state funding. One Oakland official noted that "citizens and civic organizations on this side of the bay are becoming a little tired of being neglected in the allocation of highway funds and in the matter of improved highway design."[16] In 1954, the Oakland Chamber of Commerce called for a "militant county-wide campaign" to "topple barriers" and expedite the advancement of "Metropolitan Oakland," their term for the East Bay.[17] Despite these early fears, the freeway system in the East Bay was largely completed as planned with only minor skirmishes with opposing residents, businesses, and politicians.[18]

In light of East Bay highway progress, a 1954 study by the San Francisco Chamber of Commerce concluded that without similar aggressiveness the city would no longer be the "heart of the Bay Area."[19] San Francisco planners, politicians, and businessmen were most concerned about downtown and its decline should traffic and residents shift in sizeable numbers across the Bay. Traffic entering San Francisco by crossing the Bay Bridge increased from 28.9 million vehicles in 1950 to 37.9 in 1960.[20] Planners feared traffic congestion would cause the migration of businesses away from the city. The city planning department called downtown the city's "symbolic heart" and concluded that "its fate is the fate of San Francisco."[21]

In 1951 the San Francisco city planning department adopted a traffic plan that included freeways connecting the Bay Bridge and the Golden Gate Bridge along the waterfront and through Golden Gate Park, as well as freeways connecting the city to growing peninsula cities (Figure 2). Included in the plan was the "southern crossing," or second Bay Bridge that was not built. Opposition to the 1951 plan arose immediately. The city's park commission criticized the plan for running a freeway through Golden Gate Park. Residents near the park formed the Property Owners' Association to oppose the expressway. The movement soon spread to other parts of the city. In December of 1955, more than 2,000 residents of the West Portal Home Owners' Association met with representatives of the California Division of Highways to voice their concerns. This was followed by a meeting held at Lincoln High, which attracted over 1,600 in April of 1956.[22]

The proposed freeways crossed many neighborhoods that were well organized, thereby ensuring protests. But the success of the revolt was not inevitable. What made the movement powerful was the fact that the neighborhoods supported each other's protests. Neighborhood associations had formed in the city as early as the 1850s. After the earthquake and fire, neighborhoods mobilized to ensure they received their share of reconstruction funds and services.[23] By the 1950s, nearly every city district possessed a neighborhood association.[24] Because all were organized, freeway opponents in one area received support from other districts. Each community felt threatened by the proposed freeways and did not want planners forced to bypass one area to then locate the freeway through their neighborhood.[25]

At these meetings, residents argued that freeways displaced those who had struggled for many years to buy and maintain their houses. Residents described planners as elitists who failed to sympathize with their struggles to buy a house. They had "saved and slaved" and were then told to "get out of the way of the bulldozers and 'progress.'" Freeways

Figure 2.
Trafficways Plan, San Francisco, 1951

did not just displace people but undermined everything that made up a community, including "homes, churches, and businesses."[26]   A nearby freeway caused property values to decline by 20 percent. Moreover, residents remaining in the city paid higher taxes as the expressways eliminated valuable industrial real estate from the tax roles.[27]   Chris D. McKeon, a developer, criticized the planned Western Freeway for diminishing property values in western San Francisco. He headed the Property Owners' Association, which sponsored meetings calling for the elimination of the freeway.[28] McKeon presided over a raucous neighborhood meeting in December of 1955 attended by San Francisco city planner James R. McCarthy. McCarthy complained that the meeting only served to "enflame" residents and made no attempt at "getting the facts." At the meeting, critics complained that the Western Freeway would take $13 million off the tax roles. One participant asked, "Why wreck our homes for traffic coming from outside the city."[29]

Such meetings led to homeowner petition drives that encouraged the San Francisco Board of Supervisors to vote in January of 1959 to oppose state plans for the Western, Junipero Serra, Mission, Crosstown, and Southern freeways, and the extension of the Embarcadero Freeway. The resolution specifically criticized freeways because of their impact on homeowners and neighborhoods rather than their aesthetic impact or the fact they brought cars, smog, and noise to the city. Freeway construction "involves the demolition of homes, the destruction of residential areas, the forced uprooting and relocation of individuals, families, and business enterprises," read the city supervisors' resolution. "The property taken from the tax rolls will shrink the already restricted taxable area of San Francisco—adding to a marked degree—to the already heavy burden of the taxpayers."[30]

Besides organizing to defend their homes, residents were also concerned with protecting historic city landmarks. The freeways not only threatened homes, they also threatened the city's urban culture. Two historic icons, the Ferry Building and Golden Gate Park, became battlegrounds for the preservation of San Francisco history. The battle to save these spaces from the freeways represented a fight to defend the city's urbanism against the encroaching suburban culture.

SAN FRANCISCO'S URBAN IDENTITY

Critics portrayed the attempt to build freeways in the city as the invasion of an alien suburban culture that conflicted with the urbanism of San Francisco. Since the gold rush, San Franciscans believed that their city was a special place. The city's rapid rise despite its inhospitable peninsula setting, its constant growth even after earthquakes and fires, and its world-renowned beauty made residents believe that the city was unique.

San Franciscans had clear notions about what made their city different. Residents and leaders praised San Francisco's diverse population and social tolerance, which they understood resulted from its urban character.[31]

History was a central part of the city's urban identity. Its Spanish-Mexican origins, the gold rush, the vigilantes, the cable cars and ferries, the earthquake and fire, and its phoenix-like resurrection were historical vignettes that made the city famous around the world. City elites made concerted efforts to market San Francisco's past, starting with the Midwinter Fair of 1894 and followed by the Panama-Pacific International Exposition in 1915. During the 1930s, the city sponsored several major festivals including the Century of Commerce celebration in 1935, two celebrations marking the completion of the Golden Gate and Bay Bridges, and festivities surrounding the Golden Gate International Exposition. Each event included dramatic reenactments of the city's history. Often elites encouraged the public to wear historic costumes to dances and concerts. Decorated buildings and streets became the stage for the revival of bygone eras.[32]

These historical pageants, along with the city's natural setting, and ethnic districts like Chinatown and North Beach, suggested to many that San Francisco managed to maintain its past even as it modernized. A 1939 guidebook praised the "glamour of yesterday" that was still present in the city.[33] Another observer noted that history "clings to the city and lends charm to its atmosphere even today."[34] This belief continued after the war. The city's "youth and age both lie near the surface," stated Joseph Henry Jackson in 1953. "The San Franciscan walks arm-in-arm with his busy present and his full-packed past, brisk enough as he goes about his affairs but willing to pause and recollect the yesterdays that meet him at every corner."[35]

San Francisco's seeming ability to mix past and present sprang from several factors. The city's beauty attracted scores of tourists whose presence encouraged the maintenance of authentic historic sites and the creation of new ones. As San Francisco grew, its hills remained visible, at least before World War II, providing views of the Bay and ocean, islands and mountains. The hills stalled the replacement of the cable cars with more modern forms of transportation, at least until the late 1940s. Chinatown remained stable as new immigrants augmented the population. Though rebuilt after the 1906 earthquake, architects reproduced new versions of old Chinese storefronts, and the city's geography maintained the compact district's enclosed ethnic ambiance.[36]

San Francisco recalled a European city, especially in contrast to Los Angeles. Located at the tip of a peninsula, entrepreneurs built vertically in downtown from the late 1800s, and the city enthusiastically embraced tall structures and apartment living to cope with the shortage of land.[37] In

1933 a commentator praised San Francisco as "one of the few 'skyline' cities of the nation."[38] Its urban identity intensified after World War II as its downtown became more dense. Between 1955 and 1962, office buildings represented 67 percent of the city's non-residential con- struction. San Francisco's square footage of office space was exceeded only by New York, Chicago, and Los Angeles. The city had a vacancy rate equal to New York's, but much lower than either Los Angeles or Chicago.[39]

The density of downtown construction and geographic restrictions encouraged the use of mass transit. In 1969, just over half of all city trips were taken by automobile, compared to 75 percent for the whole Bay Area. Every day, the city's mass transit system accounted for 440,000 trips, the most of any system in the Bay region, even though the Municipal Railway served only the city of San Francisco.[40] By the 1960s, however, more cars than ever were streaming into the city from the suburbs. The number of cars driven by commuters from Marin County increased by 75 percent over that decade. Overall, cars entering the city increased by 50 percent during the 1960s.[41]

The city's urbanism also encouraged social tolerance. From its earliest days, it was a youthful city. In the 1850s, after the gold rush, single migrants and immigrants of younger ages predominated. This continued as settlers tended to be single and younger in the twentieth century as well. After World War II, among the largest 12 cities in the nation, San Francisco had the highest percentage of households with one/two persons, and the lowest proportion of families. In 1950, it had the lowest percentage of families of any big city in the nation.[42]

The growth of minority communities after the war enhanced its reputation as a tolerant city. Between 1940 and 1960, many African Americans, Latinos, and Asians arrived, making non-white minorities more than 18 percent of the city's population. The African American population increased from just over 4,000 in 1940 to 43,502 in 1950 as defense jobs attracted blacks during World War II.[43] The arrival of new Latino groups who settled in the Mission District compounded the city's ethnic diversity. As early as the 1930s, gays and lesbians had established bars and restaurants in and around the North Beach area and by the 1950s and 1960s the city had gained a reputation as a gay oasis.[44]

San Franciscans tolerated not just people but also vice, which confirmed that it had modernized while maintaining its gold rush spirit. In the nineteenth century, commentators cited Chinatown and the Barbary Coast as examples of the city's acceptance of a degree of lawlessness.[45] In 1938, members of the city's police department were accused of receiving payoffs to protect houses of prostitution. The city's district attorney hired a federal G-man, Edwin Atherton, to investigate. A frustrated Atherton finally announced that although he had collected ample evidence of wrong doing, the city "wanted a so-called 'open town'" and so tolerated vice as much as did New York or New Orleans.[46]

San Francisco's maritime origins, rapid growth, numerous singles and young families, and diverse population made tolerance part of its national and international reputation. City elites publicized San Francisco's tolerance and used it to promote tourism. "If we were to describe San Francisco with a word, that word would be 'tolerant,'" noted a tourism firm during World War II. "Here is a spirit of live and let live that the world might study."[47] The longstanding prejudice faced by many Asians, blacks, gays, and Mexicans challenged that simple pronouncement. Nevertheless, a celebrated tradition of tolerance was an essential part of the city's identity.

Social tolerance, ethnic diversity, and growth that managed to combine past and present were all essential parts of the city's urban culture. Residents and elites would judge freeways and redevelopment plans based on their presumed impact on the city's culture.[48]

THE SUBURBAN THREAT TO SAN FRANCISCO'S CULTURE

Changes in the city after World War II undermined the city's ability to maintain a balance between historic preservation and modernization, and seemed to undercut its tolerance as well. All these changes suggested the city was losing its urban distinction and becoming suburbanized. The growth of the whole Bay Area during the war meant that afterward many more workers commuted to San Francisco by automobile greatly increasing downtown congestion.[49]

Adapting San Francisco to the automobile was difficult especially with the cable cars still operating up and down the steep hills. While a welcomed reminder of the city's past many city officials saw them as obstacles to an efficient transit system.[50] In 1944, the city elected a new mayor, Roger Lapham, who owned the American Hawaiian Steamship Company. During the campaign, the businessman vowed to run the city more efficiently.[51] In January of 1947, Lapham "committed political suicide," according to one observer, by stating that the city would replace the cable car lines with motorized buses. His plan outraged many city residents.[52] Undaunted, Lapham drove an old horsecar down Market Street to demonstrate that progress required that the outdated cable cars be replaced. But, consistent with San Francisco's culture, residents immediately demanded that the city not only keep the cable cars but also bring back the old horsecars.[53]

Mrs. Frieda Hans Klussman, wife of a San Francisco surgeon, proclaimed that eliminating the cable cars would be like "ripping the heart out of the city." She formed the Citizens' Committee to Save the Cable Cars and launched a referendum drive to block Lapham's plans, the first city-wide neighborhood movement that targeted City Hall. She gained the support of the Native Daughters of the Golden West and the Central Council of Civic Improvement Clubs, the latter of which represented 47 neighborhood and civic organizations. Her referendum, which won 70 percent approval, wrote two cable car lines into the city charter ensuring their survival. But the issue arose again in the mid 1950s when the city proposed cutting back on all but a couple of cable car lines. Again, Klussman organized public protests to maintain many of the lines proposed for elimination (Photo 1).[54]

The movement to eliminate the cable cars was directly related to the influence of the automobile and the suburbs. The city's Public Utilities Commission had voted to eliminate the cable car lines in order to build a parking garage on O'Farrell Street in downtown San Francisco at the behest of nearby department store owners.[55] A 1954 study concluded that traffic congestion "discourages patronage of downtown stores," and

Photo 1.
Save the Cable Cars Rally, San Francisco, 1947. Photograph courtesy of the San Francisco History Center, San Francisco Public Library.

city customers were driving to "outlying shopping centers which provide large amounts of free parking space."[56] The city's planning department had begun to look to the suburban mall as its model for downtown redevelopment. A San Francisco planning study in 1955 noted that "in terms of general attractiveness and compact arrangement, the best example of planned shopping centers can serve as a guide to modernization and renewal of downtown." The authors praised the uniform storefronts in suburban strip mall, and maintained that the variety and disunity of the city's shopping areas created "confusion and clutter." The authors also praised the design of suburban malls for separating automobiles and pedestrians. The downtown needed "courts, malls, arcades, passages, terraces, and bridges separating buildings" to create a mall-like, pedestrian-friendly shopping experience in which the consumer was not intimidated by large office buildings and traffic.[57]

Freeways were another force seemingly suburbanizing the city. While planners and department store owners felt the expressways would help the city compete with the suburbs, state highway engineers saw the city's freeways as part of a statewide transportation network. But many San Franciscans associated freeways with suburbanites who were simply passing through or temporarily visiting the city. One state engineer noted that freeways served workers traveling from "suburban homes to occupational centers."[58] Such statements only increased feelings in San Francisco that expressways served outsiders.

City planners tried to convince residents that freeways benefited locals as well as suburbanites.[59] But part of the local enmity toward freeways stemmed from the belief that they served wealthy suburbanites who had fled the city. The small towns located across the Golden Gate Bridge, like Marin and Sausalito, were home to many upper class residents. One freeway opponent concluded that state engineers "just want to enable people in Marin to visit friends in San Mateo County."[60] Thus, San Franciscans rejected the notion that they should suffer to make life more convenient for wealthy outsiders.

By the late 1950s, the suburbs had become the focus of negative national media criticism. Suburbanites were portrayed as conformist and materialistic, living in mass-produced developments that leveled hillsides and filled valleys with tract homes that excluded non-whites.[61] Some San Franciscans feared that freeways brought these suburban traits to a city that had prided itself on its urbanism. San Francisco had historically contrasted itself not only with suburbs, but with other American cities. Herb Caen, the *Chronicle*'s revered columnist, stated he was "fighting to save his city—his unique, his beloved, his personal city—from the ever-increasing onslaughts by manic-progressives, with their shopping centers, their housing projects, their freeways, and their plasticized examples of split-level thinking."[62] While Herb Caen was a romantic city booster, others also saw the freeways as a threat to the culture of the city and rebelled against the expressways.

THE EMBARCADERO FREEWAY AND THE FERRY BUILDING

The 1951 Trafficways Plan included the Embarcadero Freeway connecting the Bay Bridge and the Golden Gate Bridge along the waterfront. The San Francisco Harbor Commission and historic preservationists demanded that the freeway run underground in front of the Ferry Building. The state highway commission responded that the cost was prohibitive.[63] Moreover, the state's engineers insisted that the anticipated traffic necessitated a double-decked elevated structure. But since the area was predominantly industrial and because the Embarcadero was one of the first freeways built in the city, state engineers overcame opposition and completed the initial sections in 1959. However, neighborhood groups succeeded in blocking its extension through Telegraph Hill and the Marina District, so the freeway ended abruptly at Broadway in downtown San Francisco.

The double-decked Embarcadero Freeway obliterated the view of the Ferry Building down Market Street (Photo 2). Completed in 1898, the venerable Ferry Building had been the embarkation point for ferry commuters traveling to and from San Francisco from the East Bay and Marin, until the boats temporarily stopped running in the mid 1950s.[64] Over 50 million ferry passengers traveled through the building during the 1920s, making it the busiest transit station in the United States.[65] These commuters gave San Francisco's downtown much of its economic dynamism, and the Ferry Building symbolized its urban greatness. After arriving at the Ferry Building commuters walked to nearby stores and offices or take cable cars or streetcars to other destinations. The stately structure spoke of urban sophistication and announced the city's dominant position in the Bay Area and the state.

Built from 1896 to 1898, its architect, Arthur Page Brown, worked in the Spanish revival style popular during the late 1800s in California. After Brown died, his assistant, Willis Polk, completed the building.[66] Polk viewed the Ferry Building as a symbol of the city's historic determination to overcome the geographic barriers limiting its growth. The building "will emblazon the achievement of San Francisco upon all of the succeeding ages," said Polk, "keeping ever eternal the record of our struggles to the greatest success, fought with infinite fortitude."[67]

The new building replaced the original structure erected by the Central Pacific Railroad in 1875. The old building was but a shed where horsecars, cable cars, and ferries met. The new edifice, with its classical exterior columns, arcade and marble interior, was a substantial building that marked the entrance to downtown. It included meeting rooms and exhibit halls.   The Pacific Commercial Museum on the second floor displayed products of the nations bordering on the Pacific Ocean, signaling that world trade was an important part of the city's economy.[68] On the first floor entrance, a mosaic of the state seal pointed to places around California with the city situated at the center of the state and the Bay Area.   Thus, the Ferry Building marked the city as a destination, a center of the Bay Area metropolis.

The Ferry Building's monumental architecture reflected the city's appreciation for aesthetics in building design.   Critics believed that the Embarcadero Freeway not only obscured the Ferry Building and the view of the Bay from Market Street but also would diminish the city's appreciation for architecture more generally.

Why did the city feel so vulnerable to the effect of the freeway?   San Francisco began as an "instant city" in which rapid growth meant its first settlers looked to create a credible urban environment.[69]   In the early years, builders modeled buildings after East Coast edifices to announce

Photo 2.
The Embarcadero Freeway and the Ferry Building, 1960. Photo courtesy of the San Francisco History Center, San Francisco Public Library.

the city's bright future. Its nineteenth century buildings proved San Francisco was "boldly marching on in the race for city greatness."[70] The city's social diversity and wide-open democracy encouraged ethnic groups to express their political and social equality in ethnic architecture.[71]

After 1906, architecture spurred local confidence in the city's revival after the disastrous earthquake and fire.[72] Willis Polk's Hallidie Building (1918), with its glass facade, expressed the city's risk taking spirit, defying those skeptics who feared it was susceptible to another temblor or conflagration.[73]   Polk himself stated that the post-1906 buildings represented "the spirit of San Francisco, the ambitious commercial spirit of a place."[74]

Polk and other San Francisco elites around the turn of the century viewed architecture as a tool for unifying the city's diverse populace. In 1905, the city hired Daniel H. Burnham to create a city plan that would provide residents with a greater sense of common attachment to the city and appreciation for their democratic responsibilities.   Burnham's plan called for a civic center composed of buildings in the monumental classicist style connected to wide boulevards, which provided great vistas of the symbols of government. The civic center included city hall, the opera house, and the main library. Burnham followed the City Beautiful precepts which grew from the 1893 World's Columbian Exposition in Chicago. The fair's White City expressed the view held by some elites that by the late-nineteenth century, the materialism born out of industrial capitalism had obscured the civic responsibilities of both workers and employers.[75]   Planners and architects concluded that much of labor unrest, urban crime, violence, disease, and poverty resulted from poor housing, schools, and lack of public amenities like public parks and community centers. They believed that by reforming the built environ-ment they would educate all citizens about their responsibilities to each other within a democratic republic.[76]

The 1906 earthquake and fire created the opportunity to implement Burnham's plan for San Francisco. But infighting among businessmen who desired to rebuild as quickly as possible eliminated any large-scale remodeling of the city. Only the civic center, built between 1915 and 1926 would conform to the Burnham plan.

The Ferry Building, though built before the earthquake, reflected City Beautiful ideals. Both Arthur Page Brown and Willis Polk had worked with Burnham. Brown had designed the California building at the 1893 Chicago Columbian Exposition, and Polk worked with Burnham in Chicago and assisted him on his plan for San Francisco. Polk was disappointed in the city's failure to implement the plan, and he later designed a Burnham-influenced columned entrance to the Ferry Building that was never constructed.[77]

Criticism of the Embarcadero Freeway's obliteration of the view of the

Ferry Building reflected the edifice's role as an expression of the city's spirit and history. By blocking views of the Ferry Building from Market Street, the freeway undermined the hope that through respect for the built environment the city could uphold San Francisco's ideals of unity, tolerance, and responsible citizenship.

The *Chronicle* and others continually demanded that the completed Embarcadero Freeway be razed. The concern about aesthetics took place precisely when the city appeared to be pulling apart, as white flight was followed by the growth of entrenched ghettos. In the face of these occurrences, the city's traditional unifying culture was being undermined through the importation of suburban landscapes. The danger of growing alienation from the cityscape was made clear in the series of urban riots that reduced several black neighborhoods to smoldering ruins across the country.

The suburbanization of the city suggested it was losing its historic culture and tolerance. The Embarcadero Freeway was assailed for destroying the city's sense of "esthetic values" that preserved order and united the population.[78] A concern for good design had bound residents to the city and heightened concern for its citizens. The freeway not only obliterated views of the Ferry Building but it also undermined the city's ability to bind a citizenry to a common culture. In so doing, San Francisco was made more like the suburbs, lacking in tolerance and any sense of history.

Freeway advocates tried to rectify the situation by creating a new space that would bring San Franciscans together. Mayor George Christopher proposed that a park be constructed around the Ferry Building and under the elevated freeway. "No park can hope to hide the monstrous ugliness of the Embarcadero Freeway," noted the *Chronicle*. "The only solution was to tear it down, and give the Ferry Building and the celebrated view of the bay back to the city."[79] Giving the view back to all residents would mean giving back to them that which had bound them together—their love for the city's beauty and history.

Supporters of the freeway scoffed at the notion that the views of the harbor and waterfront or the Ferry Building were worth preserving. The *San Francisco Examiner* insisted that the wharves and cranes along the docks already obscured the Bay view, and that the Ferry Building was "one of the city's most historic but least aesthetic structures."[80]

This conflict arose while the city was making a difficult shift from an industrial/commercial economy to one focused on finance and tourism. The conflict over the Embarcadero Freeway and the Ferry Building reflected the difficult process of economic transformation. The decline of the city's maritime industry in the 1950s and 1960s produced questions about the waterfront's purpose. Should the city struggle to revive its shipping economy or should the waterfront serve other purposes perhaps as a tourist area? Many valued the waterfront as an industrial/warehousing site. One writer wondered, "Do they want us to sweep away our docks and substitute greensward for busy shipping?"[81]

But that is precisely what some advised Mayor George Christopher, including developers who anticipated building new shops, offices, and apartments in the embarcadero area. Gerald O'Hara, president of the San Francisco Planning and Housing Association, said the Embarcadero Freeway will "make the area . . . a colossal eyesore" that would thwart attempts to rejuvenate the waterfront.[82]

Opposition came from different angles, yet criticism of the Embarcadero Freeway expressed the desire to maintain the city's urbanism. Redevelopers called for building new high-rise apartments and office buildings on the waterfront but the freeway interfered. Others said the freeway undermined the city's ability to maintain civic unity by obscuring an important symbol of the city's urban history and culture. Still others felt the freeway further weakened the city's role as the primary Bay Area metropolis. The freeway suggested the city had become a throughway and not a destination. Finally, many opposed the freeway for making the city conform to suburban architecture, which prized the road over preserving historic structures and views.[83]

SAVING GOLDEN GATE PARK

The Embarcadero Freeway's ugliness spurred the anti-freeway movement. After the supervisors voted to eliminate six of nine freeways in January of 1959, state engineers and city planners began looking at Golden Gate Park as a route that would not force as many residents to relocate. But targeting the park produced an outpouring of criticism from environmentalists, homeowners, and politicians. The park embodied two elements deemed intrinsic to the city's culture: democracy and history. Freeway opponents argued that the park was built for the people of the city, and so residents should determine its treatment, not the state engineers who had no sense for the importance of the park to the city's history and culture.

City planners first suggested a freeway route through the park in 1954. The city's Recreation and Parks Commission rallied support for the park's defense. Led by Commission President Louis Sutter and Commissioner Ann Dippel, the city agency formed a "Keep the Freeways Out of the Park Committee" and met with city leaders to quash the idea.[84] The freeway threatened an eight-block section that served originally as the carriage entrance to the park. Perhaps because it was the park's original entrance or the first section developed, the Panhandle contained over 50 varieties of trees from California, the United States, and throughout the world.[85]

Defending Golden Gate Park from the Panhandle Freeway became linked to the environmental movement of the early 1960s.   In San Francisco, the ecology movement concentrated on saving the bay from overdevelopment, air and water pollution, and restricting urban sprawl.[86] If freeway construction continued, a San Francisco radio newsman noted, San Francisco would be consumed by "a ghastly combination of concrete monsters, side-by-side with immense parking garages, all of which will be overladen with the poisonous smog which is already choking the life out of us now."[87]   The obvious model for this scenario was southern California, the region to which San Franciscans had always proudly contrasted their city. Elizabeth Probert, a member of the environmental group the Sierra Club, called for the preservation of open space since "it won't be long until the entire Bay Area is one megalopolis."[88]   Another observer noted that streets, freeways, and parking lots meant two-thirds of Los Angeles was paved over, a situation that residents did not want "imposed" in the Bay Area.[89]

Besides ecological fears, plans for the Panhandle Freeway created an outcry because the park was an historic artifact.   The city park in the United States stemmed directly from urban life and was, according to the historian Gunther Barth, "an essential component of the modern city."[90]   Beginning with Central Park in New York City, designed by Frederick Law Olmsted in the mid-nineteenth century, Americans considered urban parks to be the "lungs of the city," helping to clean polluted air while providing urbanites contact with nature and a calming contrast to the surrounding competitive metropolis.   Other U.S. cities soon built central parks, which became a sign of sophisticated urbanity.[91]

Golden Gate Park had special meaning to San Franciscans. Unlike other cities, environmental realities made San Francisco particularly inhospitable for constructing an urban park.   When a park was first proposed for the wind-swept sand dunes in the city's western part in the 1850s, few believed anything could grow in such an inhospitable environment. The park's creator, William Hammond Hall, sowed barley then lupine to establish a root system in the sand able to withstand wind, drought, and fog.[92] He then planted many other grass varieties, followed by wind resistant shrubs, bushes, and trees, to further establish a foothold in the sand.[93]

The city's residents understandably praised Hall for the miracle of transforming sand dunes into a luscious park.   Because of its totally artificial origins, the park was like a painting, and Hall and John McLaren, his successor in 1887, were artists who planted each tree and shrub with the entire composition in mind.   An early commentator noted that McLaren "has the rare genius of painting upon the soil of waste places."[94] Another called him a "master artist," for turning sand dunes into a park.[95] During the Panhandle Freeway debate, Harold Gilliam, a *Chronicle* writer and freeway critic, called Golden Gate Park the city's "greatest work of art."[96]

The park was not just a place for urbanites to relax; it was also a monument to the city's history. Gilliam linked the park's various areas to important city figures and periods. McLaren planted the redwoods "nearly half a century ago," to memorialize the fallen World War I veterans. The freeway would slice through columns of oak trees, the "principal tree growing in San Francisco in the era of the explorers." The oak grove allowed residents and visitors to gain a sense of the landscape of the state "before the bulldozers," when the trees and foothills overlooked "fertile valleys still unsubdivided."[97]

Just as the fight against the Embarcadero Freeway was a struggle to maintain the city's aesthetic sense, preserving the park was seen as a battle to preserve the city's "natural heritage."[98] The freeway threatened "indigenous oaks," a "vestige of San Francisco's natural ground cover," and other spaces with historical significance, like Mountain Lake near the original settlement founded during the Juan Bautista de Anza expedition in 1776. San Franciscans identified the park with its early leaders, like William C. Walker, a nurseryman, who in the 1850s provided the park with trees, bushes, and plants. Walker also initiated the first large planting of eucalyptus trees in the city.[99] Losing the park's trees lessened the city's ability to value nature in general.[100]

While seeking to defend the park as an embodiment of the city's history, Gilliam assailed what he termed the "engineering mind," which valued only saving time and money and devalued nature and the past. The "slide rule calculations" by engineers could not factor in the social effects of the freeways. The state highway engineers called for relocating the Panhandle trees, which Gilliam found unacceptable because the trees were part of an ecological unit. "It is not individual trees . . . that compose a woods," he insisted. "It is the total setting—hills, swales and natural terrain that make up a woodland atmosphere."[101] He called for including "social welfare specialists, housing experts, social psychologists, community relations professionals" in studies of freeway locations.[102]

The park's association with democracy, which San Franciscans particularly valued as part of the city's history, drew defenders. Hall and McLaren were common men who labored to build a park for all residents. Wealthy philanthropists donated funds for trees that all city residents enjoyed. This democratic reputation informed freeway opposition. The park, said one freeway opponent, was "a legacy given to the people of San Francisco."[103] Commentators noted that the poorer residents now living in the nearby Haight district had no other park and so they used the Panhandle as a neighborhood playground.[104]

Urban riots in other cities in the early 1960s intensified feelings that the city needed to assist the poor, not undermine their environment.

Gilliam noted that the freeway would also displace 1,200 black residents in the Western Addition. "How many times do you roust people out of their homes—particularly members of minority groups who have trouble finding housing elsewhere?" He argued that mental health experts, grassroots activists, and social service providers should determine freeway routes.[105]   The park would have a direct role in social welfare by employing minority children and providing recreational programs in 1967.[106]

The movement to save the park became an expression of grassroots democracy. Opponents of the freeway helped form the Citizens' Planning Commission, which considered new projects throughout the city. The Commission's president, Albert E. Meakin, was also co-chair of the "Committee to Save Golden Gate Park."[107]   Historically, urban parks have been meeting places for organizing dissent.[108]   Opponents of the Panhandle Freeway held a rally at the Golden Gate Park polo field on May 17, 1964. The rally was sponsored by a citizens' committee representing 26 civic and neighborhood groups. The rally served to identify the freeway with the dictatorial culture of outsiders who were attempting to foist a foreign suburban culture onto the city. Speakers assailed the supporters of the "cement octopus" and noted the origins of freeways in Sacramento and the difficulty local residents had in getting design alterations or in blocking construction.[109]   Fighting powerful bureaucrats demanded unified civic participation. "Politics should be everyone's business," said one speaker. "Elected officers have influence on jobs, housing, and even choice of freeways. If more people who are interested in stronger voices in government got into politics we would have a better political system."[110]   Speakers portrayed state engineers as dictators who answered to no one. While the engineers gave San Franciscans the right to accept or reject the freeway, the city had no power to shape its design.[111]

Freeway opponents also defended the nearby Haight neighborhood from disruption. By the early 1960s, the Haight was becoming known as a place for non-conformists. The Haight, which bordered on Golden Gate Park, for many years embodied the city's cosmopolitan character.[112] In the 1940s, it was home to numerous labor union activists, and one resident remembered it as a "working class residential district with a liberal and progressive atmosphere." By the 1960s, the Haight had evolved into a bohemian, working class, racially mixed neighborhood. Between 1950 and 1960, the Haight's black population grew from 2 to 17 percent. Blacks displaced by redevelopment in the Filmore neighborhood relocated to the Haight where rents were cheap and they were accepted by old-timers.[113]   The Haight was also home for many San Francisco State students, the so-called "beatniks" forced out of North Beach by downtown development and police harassment, and Chinese and

Filipinos.[114] To add to the mix, several gay bars and a gay theater opened in the early 1960s.[115]

In 1959, Haight residents formed the Haight Ashbury Neighborhood Council (HANC) which opposed urban redevelopment and the freeway.[116] The HANC made maintaining an integrated neighborhood one of its primary goals. The Haight's diversity was recognized and valued by residents throughout the city. One opponent argued that the worst potential impact of the Panhandle Freeway was the undermining of the city's "best integrated neighborhood of minority groups."[117]

In 1966, the city's supervisors voted down the Panhandle Freeway 6-5. Opponents wearing hats with signs that read "Save Us from the Freeway" packed the meeting and cheered with every "No" vote registered. The freeway opponents upheld the "spirit" of the city by standing up to the powerful state highway lobby. The freeway battle over the park became a struggle to define the place of democracy in the city. Freeway supporters believed that mob action had displaced those transportation experts whose training and expertise equipped them with the ability to make decisions about freeways. "While 'Save the Park' enthusiasts today abandon themselves in the Golden Gate Park polo field to the joy of fighting freeways," said an *Examiner* writer, "scores of worried public officials and professionals will be doing their homework on the last Panhandle Parkway plan."[118] Before the supervisors voted, industrialist Louis Ets-Hokin proclaimed, "Your vote today . . . will tell the people of San Francisco whether they have a constitutional government . . . or a body controlled by mob rule, a very vociferous, vigilante-type minority comprised of pseudo-intellectuals, self-service publicity seekers and plain jackasses."[119] The Embarcadero Freeway stood as a model of the highway men's "one-track, four lane minds," which valued nothing other than efficiency. Their insensitivity to the city and its history led residents to rally to defend Golden Gate Park, a symbol of the city's urbanism.

CONCLUSION

The culture wars are seen as emanating from debates in Congress over religion, education, the family, the media, and sexuality. But the battle to preserve San Francisco's urbanism also represented a clash of cultures. The battle pitted San Francisco's urban culture against the harbinger of the suburban lifestyle, the freeway. After World War II, Americans held sharply divided views about cities and suburbs. The popular media lauded suburbs as good places to raise families, while scholars portrayed them as conformist, homogeneous, materialistic, and exclusive. At the same time, city and suburb converged in important ways. Whites fled the city for the suburbs, shifting political and economic power to the hinterlands. The city tried to emulate the suburbs by turning downtown into a shopping mall and trying to accommodate motorists. In San Francisco, planners eliminated several cable car lines and pushed for new parking garages and freeways.

But planners ran up against San Francisco's reputation as a "special place" that had managed to remain a cosmopolitan city that was tolerant of diversity and respectful of history. Before World War II, visitors praised the city's ability to merge past and present. Chinatown, North Beach, the cable cars, and the ferries recalled old San Francisco even as the city modernized. Similarly, the city's hills and fog linked San Franciscans of the twentieth century to those of the nineteenth century.

But by the 1950s, the city seemed unable to continue to build new structures while also preserving reminders of the past. Developers leveled hills to construct new subdivisions. A citizen movement resisted the elimination of the cable car lines, but ultimately only a couple of routes were preserved, largely for tourists. Chinatown continued to grow because of new immigration, yet the Italian flavor of North Beach declined as younger Italians moved out. Increased air pollution threatened to replace the city's famous fog. In the mid 1950s, the ferries stopped plying the Bay between Oakland and San Francisco.

As the automobile threatened these symbols of old San Francisco, opposition to the freeways mounted. The expressways further heralded a break with the city's ability to merge past and present. The freeways assaulted two historic icons: the Ferry Building and Golden Gate Park. By allowing more cars to enter the city, the freeways foretold a future of traffic congestion, parking garages, air pollution, and further erosion of the city's historic landscapes. Suburbanization of the city seemed to be inevitable.

The fight against the freeways was won as city elites concluded that traffic congestion required rapid transit. With the completion of the Bay Area Rapid Transit (BART) in the early 1970s, high-rises proliferated in downtown San Francisco. Residents largely embraced these buildings because they reinforced the city's urban identity. The high-rises also buttressed San Francisco's image as *the* center of the Bay Area, even as its population declined relative to the other centers in the multicentered metropolis.[120] San Franciscans supported BART because the system confirmed that the city was once again a destination. In contrast, the freeways threatened to diminish the city's standing by making it one more stop in the regional expressway network. Urban residents outside San Francisco, however, saw BART as a sign of the increasing power of the suburbs over their urban neighborhoods. In the poorer community of West Oakland, resistance developed against BART and the growing influence of the suburbs.

NOTES

1. James Q. Wilson, "Cars and Their Enemies," *Commentary* 104 (July 1997): 17–23.

2. Julia Meaton and David Morrice, "The Ethics and Politics of Private Automobile Use," *Environmental Ethics* 18 (Spring 1996): 39–54.

3. See William Sharpe and Leonard Wallock, "Bold New City or Built up 'Burb'? Redefining Contemporary Suburbia," *American Quarterly* 46 (March 1994): 1–29.

4. See James J. Flink, *The Car Culture* (Cambridge, 1975).

5. "Letters to the Editor," *Commentary* 104 (October 1997): 5.

6. Kenneth T. Jackson, *Crabgrass Frontier: The Suburbanization of the United States* (New York, 1985), 246–271.

7. Clay McShane, *Down the Asphalt Path: The Automobile and the American City* (New York, 1994), 149–171.

8. John B. Rae, *The Road and the Car in American Life* (Cambridge, 1971), 167.

9. Wilson, "Cars and Their Enemies," 19.

10. For a spirited refutation of the view that suburbs harm cities, see Brett W. Hawkins and Stephen L. Percy "On Anti-Suburban Orthodoxy," *Social Science Quarterly* 72, no. 3 (September 1991): 478–503. See also David M. Hummon, *Commonplaces: Community Ideology and Identity in American Culture* (Albany, 1990). On intolerance, see James Davison Hunter, *Culture Wars: The Struggle to Define America* (New York, 1991), 27.

11. Jackson, *Crabgrass Frontier*, 249.

12. Richard O. Baumbach and William E. Borah, *The Second Battle of New Orleans* (Tuscaloosa, 1991); Gordon Fellman, *The Deceived Majority* (New Brunswick, 1973); Alan Lupo et al., *Rites of Way* (Boston, 1971); Helen Leavitt, *Superhighway-Superhoax* (Garden City, 1970); James H. Banks, "Protest and Transportation Policy: The Freeway Disputes" (unpublished paper, ITS, 1969).

13. See Mel Scott, *The San Francisco Bay Area: A Metropolis in Perspective*, 2d ed. (Berkeley, 1985), 50, 57–70.

14. Miller McClintock, *A Report on the Street Traffic Control Problems of San Francisco* (San Francisco, 1927), 83.

15. "Bay Region Transit Problems," *Transactions of the Commonwealth Club of California* 31 (June 29, 1937): 385–387.

16. *Oakland Post-Enquirer*, November 8, 1941.

17. Oakland Chamber of Commerce, *The Future Is Now: A Report on Alameda County* (Oakland, 1954), 1.

18. See *Oakland Tribune*, April 9, 1954; *San Francisco Chronicle*, March 26, 1958.

19. San Francisco Chamber of Commerce, *Construction Projects for the State Highways in the City and County of San Francisco, 1955-1956* (San Francisco, 1954), 1.

20. Paul F. Wendt, *Dynamics of Central City Land Values, San Francisco and Oakland, 1950 to 1960* (Berkeley, 1961), 23.

21. San Francisco Department of City Planning, *Modernizing Downtown San Francisco* (San Francisco, 1955), 5.

22. See William H. Lathrop, Jr., "San Francisco Freeway Revolt," *Transportation Engineering Journal: Proceedings of the American Society of Civil Engineers* 97 (February 1971): 134–136.

23. Judd Kahn, *Imperial San Francisco: Politics and Planning in an American City, 1897-1906* (Lincoln, 1979), 206.

24. Stephen E. Barton, "A History of the Neighborhood Movement in San Francisco," *Berkeley Planning Journal* 2, nos. 1-2 (Spring-Fall 1985): 85–105.

25. Lathrop, "San Francisco Freeway Revolt," 142.

26.   *San Francisco Call-Bulletin*, April 26, 1956.

27.   *Chronicle*, March 26, 1954.

28.   *Chronicle*, June 1, 1956.

29.   Memo from James R. McCarthy to Paul Opperman on Lincoln Community Association Meeting (December 12, 1955); misc. materials, freeway revolt, SFHC.

30.   Lathrop, "San Francisco Freeway Revolt," 139.

31.   See Robert W. Cherny, "Patterns of Toleration and Discrimination in San Francisco: The Civil War to World War I," *California History* 72 (Summer 1994): 131–140. See also Howard S. Becker, ed., *Culture and Civility in San Francisco* (Chicago, 1971).

32.   Gunther Barth, *Instant Cities: Urbanization and the Rise of San Francisco and Denver* (Albuquerque, 1988), 202–203; William Issel and Robert W. Cherny, *San Francisco, 1865-1932: Politics, Power, and Urban Development* (Berkeley, 1986), 167–170.

33.   See Edith Shelton and Elizabeth Field, *Let's Have Fun in San Francisco* (San Francisco, 1939), 21.

34.   "Historical San Francisco," unpublished paper, San Francisco Chamber of Commerce, San Francisco, 1939; CHS.

35.   Joseph Henry Jackson, *My San Francisco* (New York, 1953), 2.

36.   On Chinatown, see Ivan Light, "From Vice District to Tourist Attraction: The Moral Career of American Chinatowns, 1880-1940," *Pacific Historical Review* 43, no. 3 (August 1974): 367–394; Ruth Hall Whitfield, "Public Opinion and the Chinese Question in San Francisco, 1900-1947" (master's thesis, University of California-Berkeley, 1940); Gunther Barth, *Bitter Strength: A History of the Chinese in the United States, 1850-1870* (Cambridge, 1964); Judy Yung, *Unbound Feet: A Social History of Chinese Women in San Francisco* (Berkeley, 1995).

37.   Michael Maurice O'Shaughnessy, *Report on Rapid Transit Plans for San Francisco: With Special Consideration to a Subway Under Market Street* (San Francisco, 1931), 5–9.

38.   R. B. Koeber, "Uniting the San Francisco Bay Area By Two Mammoth Bridge Projects" (unpublished paper, San Francisco Chamber of Commerce, San Francisco, 1933), 1; CHS.

39.   Arthur D. Little, Inc., *Community Renewal Programming: A San Francisco Study* (New York, 1966), 38–39.

40.   Bay Area Transportation Commission, *Bay Area Transportation Report* (San Francisco, 1969), 28, 34.

41.   See Frederick M. Wirt, *Power in the City: Decision Making in San Francisco* (Berkeley, 1974), 38.

42.   Little, Inc., *Community Renewal Programming*, 38.

43.   See Albert S. Broussard, *Black San Francisco: The Struggle for Racial Equality in the West, 1900-1954* (Lawrence, 1993); Douglas H. Daniels, *Pioneer Urbanites: A Social and Cultural History of Black San Francisco* (Philadelphia, 1980).

44.   Susan Stryker and Jim Van Buskirk, *Gay by the Bay: A History of Queer Culture in the San Francisco Bay Area* (San Francisco, 1995), 18–26; Manuel Castells, *The City and the Grassroots: A Cross-Cultural Theory of Urban Social Movements* (Berkeley, 1983), 138–169.

45.   Barth, *Instant Cities*, 145–150.

46.   See Curt Gentry, *The Madams of San Francisco: An Irreverent History of the City by the Golden Gate* (New York, 1964), 268.

47.   Californians Inc., *Your Victory Vacation in San Francisco* (San Francisco, 1944), 3.

48.   See for example Allan Temko, "San Francisco Rebuilds Again," *Harper's Magazine* (April 1960): 51–59.

49.   Richard M. Zettel, *Urban Transportation in the San Francisco Bay Area*

(Berkeley, 1963), 14.

50.   Miller McClintock, *Report on the San Francisco Citywide Traffic Survey* (San Francisco, 1937), 50–51.

51.   Roger D. Lapham, "An Interview on Shipping, Labor, San Francisco City Government, and American Foreign Aid" (transcript of interview conducted January-August 1956 by Corinne L. Gilb, Regional Cultural History Project, University of California-Berkeley, 1957), 166.

52.   Christopher Swan, *Cable Car* (Berkeley, 1973), 113.

53.   Swan, *Cable Car*, 114; Lucius Beebe and Charles Clegg, *Cable Car Carnival* (Oakland, 1951), 116.

54.   Anthony Perles, *The People's Railway: The History of the Municipal Railway of San Francisco* (Glendale, 1988), 158.

55.   Perles, *People's Railway,* 163; *Downtowner,* May 19, 1955; *Downtowner,* August 26, 1954. *Downtowner* was the official newspaper of the San Francisco Down Town Association.

56.   San Francisco Bureau of Engineering, Department of Public Works, *Report to the Parking Authority of San Francisco on a Downtown Parking Program* (San Francisco, February 1954), 9.

57.   San Francisco Department of City Planning, *Modernizing Downtown San Francisco,* 22, 38.

58.   B. W. Booker, "Bay Area Freeways," *California Highways and Public Works* 33 (March-April 1954): 1.

59.   San Francisco Department of City Planning, *Trafficways in San Francisco—A Reappraisal* (San Francisco, 1960), 4-6.

60.   *Chronicle,* April 28, 1956. See also *San Francisco News*, December 3, 1957; *Call-Bulletin,* April 26, 1956.

61.   See John Keats, *A Crack in the Picture Window* (Boston, 1956); William H. Whyte, *The Organization Man* (New York, 1956); Betty Friedan, *The Feminine Mystique* (New York, 1963).

62.   San Francisco Chronicle, *Hills of San Francisco* (San Francisco, 1959), 1.

63.   Herbert Marshall Goodwin, "California's Growing Freeway System" (Ann Arbor, 1969), 421.

64.   Today's jam-packed freeways have led to a revival of the ferries that run to the Ferry Building from the East Bay with plans for future expansion.

65.   Roger R. Olmsted and T. H. Walkins, *Here Today: San Francisco's Architectural Heritage* (San Francisco, 1968), 91.

66.   Harold Gilliam, *The San Francisco Experience* (Garden City, 1972), 34.

67.   Willis Polk Scrapbook, Environmental Design Library, University of California-Berkeley, p. 27–28.

68.   See Charles Keeler, *San Francisco and Thereabout* (San Francisco, 1906), 52.

69.   See Barth, *Instant Cities,* 195–196.

70.   *California Architect and Building News* 10 (February 15, 1889): 19.

71.   Ron Robin, *Signs of Change: Urban Iconography in San Francisco, 1880-1915* (New York, 1990), 74–75.

72.   See "San Francisco's Recuperative Energy," *Architecture and Engineering of California* 10 (October 1907): 41.

73.   "The World's First Glass Front Building," *Architect and Engineer* 53, no. 1 (April 1918): 71–73.

74.   Polk Scrapbook, 48.

75.   James Gilbert, *Perfect Cities: Chicago's Utopias of 1893* (Chicago, 1991).

76.   See Paul S. Boyer, *Urban Masses and Moral Order in America, 1820-1920* (Cambridge 1978), 270–283; William H. Wilson, *The City Beautiful Movement* (Baltimore, 1989). For San Francisco planning see Kahn, *Imperial San Francisco*; Mansel

G. Blackford, *Lost Dream: Businessmen and City Planning on the Pacific Coast, 1890-1920* (Columbus, 1993), 31–62.

77.   See Richard W. Longstreth, *On the Edge of the World: Four Architects in San Francisco at the Turn of the Century* (Cambridge, 1983), 240–244.

78.   *Chronicle*, September 24, 1956.

79.   Goodwin, "California's Growing Freeway System," 448.

80.   Quoted in Ibid., 426-427; *Examiner*, November 4, 1962.

81.   *Examiner*, December 12, 1953.

82.   Goodwin, "California's Growing Freeway System," 429–431.

83.   See James Richard Taylor, "Freeways and Major Highways in the San Francisco Bay Area" (unpublished paper, University of California-Berkeley, 1962).

84.   *Chronicle*, December 10, 1954.

85.   See Elizabeth McClintock and Virginia Moore, *Trees of the Panhandle, Golden Gate Park, Sam Francisco* (San Francisco, 1965), 3.

86.   Richard DeLuca, *"We the People!": Bay Area Activism in the 1960s: Three Case Studies* (San Bernardino, 1994), 52–55.

87.   Dan Morgan, KCBS radio editorial, September 23, 1965, misc. materials, freeway revolt, SFHC.

88.   *Chronicle*, July 11, 1964.

89.   Taylor, "Freeways and Major Highways in the San Francisco Bay Area," 10.

90.   See Gunther Barth, *Fleeting Moments: Nature and Culture in American History* (New York, 1990), 148.

91.   See Roy Rosenzweig and Elizabeth Blackmar, *The Park and the People: A History of Central Park* (Ithaca, 1992); Daniel Bluestone, *Constructing Chicago* (New Haven, 1991), 7–61; Galen Cranz, *The Politics of Park Design: A History of Urban Parks in America* (Cambridge, 1982).

92.   Barth, *Fleeting Moments*, 173.

93.   Oscar Lewis, *San Francisco: Mission to Metropolis* 2d ed. (San Diego, 1980), 161–165.

94.   George Homer Meyer et al., eds., *Municipal Blue Book of San Francisco* (San Francisco, 1915), 136.

95.   Michael M. Zarchin, *Glimpses of Jewish Life in San Francisco* 2d ed. (Oakland, 1964), 8.

96.   *Chronicle*, February 20, 1966.

97.   Ibid.

98.   *The Natural World of San Francisco* (Garden City, 1967), 14.

99.   McClintock and Moore, *Trees of the Panhandle,* 6.

100.   *Chronicle*, October 13, 1964.

101.   *Chronicle*, February 20, 1966.

102.   *Chronicle*, October 12, 1964.

103.   *Chronicle*, May 29, 1964.

104.   McClintock and Moore, *Trees of the Panhandle*, 3.

105.   *Chronicle*, October 12, 1964.

106.   Cranz, *Politics of Park Design*, 238.

107.   *Chronicle*, April 28, 1964.

108.   Cranz, *Politics of Park Design*, 237.

109.   See DeLuca, *"We the People!"*, 55.

110.   *Chronicle*, May 18, 1964; *Haight-Ashbury Independent*, May 14, 1964.

111.   *Chronicle*, March 13, 1966.

112.   See *Chronicle*, October 14, 1964. On casting the deciding vote against the freeway, San Francisco supervisor Terry Francois noted the importance of saving the "unique and enviable" character of the integrated Haight.

113.   Brian J. Godfrey, *Neighborhoods in Transition: The Making of San Francisco's*

Ethnic and Non-Conformist Communities (Berkeley, 1988), 183.

114.   See David F. Myrick, *San Francisco's Telegraph Hill* (Berkeley, 1972), 125.

115.   Sherri Cavan, *Hippies of the Haight* (St. Louis, 1972), 44–45, 55.

116.   Godfrey, *Neighborhoods in Transition*, 183, 186.

117.   Ann Purdy, "The Case Against a Freeway in Golden Gate Park," July 29, 1964; misc. materials, freeway revolt, SFHC.

118.   *Examiner*, May 17, 1964.

119.   *Examiner*, March 22, 1966.

120.   On the anti-growth movement and the fight against the high-rises, see Richard Edward DeLeon, *Left Coast City: Progressive Politics in San Francisco, 1975-1991* (Lawrence, 1992), 57–83.

2

BART AND
AFFIRMATIVE ACTION
IN WEST OAKLAND

As the culture wars indicate, Americans increasingly find themselves at odds over fundamental social values like religion, sexuality, free speech, and gender roles. But other aspects of modern American life have also generated conflicts about cultural values. For example, in making the case for a new rapid transit system, a Bay Area transportation expert in 1969 noted:

Availability of urban transportation provides workers with choices in jobs and places to live ... Travel for many purposes (shopping, recreation, social activity, education, and the like) permits us to enjoy the rewards of our economic effort. Urban mobility is one of our cherished community values to be weighed along with other values, not to be set off against them.[1]

The idea that urban mobility is "one of our cherished community values" might strike some as odd. Clearly, though, many Americans place a high value on mobility, especially as suburbs grow and the daily commutes of many workers lengthen. Not all Americans agree, however, that mobility is a "cherished community value." Some blame metropolitan mobility for destroying communities. As one Mexican American resident in Oakland stated in 1966:

Community decline ... must be blamed on progress. Rapid transit by automobiles, by rail and by air, make it possible for the householders in one city block, if they are on the proper level of income and opportunity, to relocate to different clubs, lodges, unions, associations or societies five or five hundred miles from the street on which they live.[2]

This speaker believed that modern mobility made maintaining

communities difficult.[3] In fact, many Americans do not know or interact, except superficially, with their neighbors. This is partly because they do not travel, work, or socialize together. Only when an intrusion like an influx of "outsiders" or a proposed highway or other construction project threatens their community do neighbors rally together and work toward defending their neighborhoods.

This chapter looks at the debate over the building of the Bay Area Rapid Transit (BART) in the mid 1960s. Chapter one showed how middle-class San Francisco residents mobilized against the suburbanization of their city, fighting freeways that undermined symbols of the city's cosmopolitan urbanism. This chapter describes minority residents in Oakland battling against the suburbanization of their urban community. The proponents of BART celebrated increased regional mobility and denigrated the ghetto as a site of poverty. Transit experts argued that only regional mobility would end poverty by providing the poor with access to jobs in the suburbs. Yet these arguments appeared specious to many West Oaklanders who realized that BART primarily served suburbanites commuting into downtown San Francisco and Oakland.

In contrast, black activists in West Oakland denounced the materialistic, individualistic, suburban culture that BART promoted. They argued that the system undermined their community by displacing residents and promoting the suburbanization of jobs. The ensuing argument about the costs and benefits of mobility represented a clash of different cultural perspectives. Moreover, the debate about the value of community cohesion and mobility evolved into a discussion of affirmative action. West Oakland leaders demanded that BART compensate those poor residents it displaced by hiring local minorities to build and operate the system. They argued that West Oakland was not a ghetto but a viable neighborhood where working-class people had settled after years of migration and economic hardship. Because BART undermined that community, BART had a special obligation to employ local residents.

This link between transportation and affirmative action was not unique to Oakland. Though affirmative action developed as a concept following the 1964 Civil Rights Act, early black activists had demanded employment based on the existence of predominantly black areas, and the operation of public transit through those communities. In 1955, Rosa Parks refused to give up her seat on a city bus in Montgomery, Alabama. After her arrest, Montgomery blacks boycotted the bus system, calling on the city to desegregate public transit. Besides an end to segregation, they also sought "Negro bus drivers in predominant Negro neighborhoods."[4] Thus, they demanded desegregated transit and public employment based on the fact that city buses passed through predominantly black communities in Montgomery. Without a black majority community, their argument for public employment would have carried much less weight. Blacks deserved better service, and black drivers would provide it. Similarly, in West Oakland, the presence of a large minority community, which BART disrupted, added power to the demand that BART hire more minorities.

Blacks in West Oakland demanded that BART construction contracts be let to minority firms willing to recruit and train minority laborers. BART, they believed, had a moral obligation to the West Oakland community because the politically selected route displaced poor homeowners and renters living in the area. Just like in Montgomery, the call from West Oakland for affirmative action depended on the presence of a minority community that, activists claimed, directly suffered from BART's construction.

BART officials resisted demands for an affirmative action hiring policy because they disagreed that BART harmed minorities. In fact, they argued that BART, with stations in the middle of ghetto neighborhoods, especially benefited minorities who lacked automobiles. In effect, officials believed that one of BART's benefits was providing ghetto dwellers the mobility to function in a modern, expanding regional metropolis. Since they did not believe the system was racist, they argued against special compensation for local residents. In contrast, black activists called for affirmative action because they desired that West Oakland remain a stable residential area. They believed that BART was obligated to help maintain West Oakland.

BART AND URBAN RIVALRY

Between 1940 and 1950, the Bay Area's population soared from 1.3 million to 2.1 million, while the region doubled in square miles from 304 to 685. In 1960 the Bay Area's population had reached 3.2 million covering 1,286 square miles.[5] Such rapid growth and highway congestion renewed discussions of the need for improved mass transit. In the 1930s, the Bay Bridge's construction led to talk among Oakland and San Francisco leaders of a regional rapid transit system. Businessmen in both Oakland and San Francisco feared that traffic and parking problems in their central cities would encourage residents and stores to relocate to the suburbs. Rapid transit connections to the suburbs promised to give suburban shoppers and workers continued access to downtown stores and offices.[6]

In 1947, the Joint Army-Navy Board looked at two potential locations for a second Bay Bridge. The board called for another Bay Bridge but the study also proposed an underwater rapid transit tube between San Francisco and Oakland, with trains running under San Francisco's Market Street and down the Peninsula.[7]

Following the Joint Army-Navy Board's study, San Francisco county supervisor Marvin Lewis organized a rapid transit committee to plan a regional transit authority. In 1951, the California legislature created the Bay Area Rapid Transit Commission. In 1957, the legislature passed a bill forming the Bay Area Rapid Transit District (BARTD) that included nine Bay Area counties, which was reduced to only three by the time construction began.[8]

Suburban communities were suspicious of the movement emanating from the larger cities for rapid transit and demanded that their interests receive equal consideration in planning the system. "The ideal Bay Area traffic system does NOT hinge on getting rapid transportation to and from downtown Oakland," stated a Hayward leader. "It does hinge on getting rapid transportation from one community to ANY other community in the same region."[9] Some suburban areas never were convinced that BART would benefit anyone but San Francisco and Oakland. Santa Clara County opted out because San Jose leaders believed that the automobile and freeways better suited the south bay metropolis' development plans. Eventually, due to funding problems and urban rivalries, BARTD shrunk to three counties, San Francisco, Alameda and Contra Costa County (Figure 3).

In describing and promoting BART, its advocates evidenced what might be called a suburban, middle-class, or modernist view of mobility and space. We need to appreciate this effort to "suburbanize" the city to fully understand how urban transit helped to stimulate criticism by West Oaklanders who celebrated community, cooperation, social obligations, and loyalty to neighborhood.

Urban rivalry made planning BART difficult. Oakland, San Francisco, and East Bay leaders sparred continually trying to design a system that served their local interests. In order to make BART acceptable to growing suburban communities, its supporters argued that rapid transit was a regional system suitable to the high level of integration in the Bay Area. BART would assist the movement of industry and business to the periphery so that only "finance apparatus and administrative offices" would be concentrated in Oakland and San Francisco. BART supporters promoted the idea that city and suburb were converging. "We no longer have cities at all, in the old sense. Or suburbs. What we have is a metropolitan area, or region," claimed the *San Francisco Chronicle*.[10]

The expanding region required better transit to remain a unified metropolis. Many feared the Bay Area was splitting up, particularly those leaders in Oakland and San Francisco. BART President Adrien J. Falk insisted that a region of specialized interdependent cities and suburbs was more efficient than many dispersed, self-sufficient communities. It was the "efficient aggregation of people" that produced in the United States "the highest standard of living known to man." This was because metropolitan concentration allowed Americans to take "full advantage of the division of labor in which each person contributes his special skills and abilities to the overall economic process." His disdain for the new self-sufficient "edge city" was evident. No one, he said, would want "a reversion to the economics of individualism in which each person would make his own clothing, bake his own bread and build his own house."[11]

Figure 3.
Bay Area Rapid Transit System, 1972

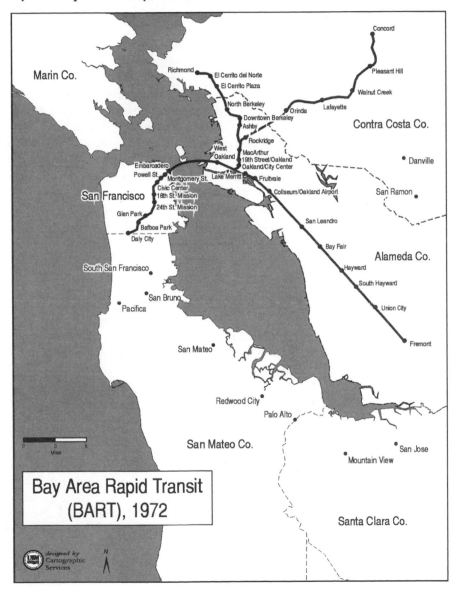

BART supporters linked increased personal freedom with the opportunity to travel quickly and comfortably throughout the region. BART would allow a person "to live where he chooses and to work where he chooses anywhere in the metropolitan area without limitations on either his choice of home or job."[12] Another proponent summed up BART's benefits as: "Freedom from the necessity to change homes when changing jobs, freedom from crowded and polluting freeways, freedom to enjoy a sports event in one city and dinner in another, freedom to live in the suburbs and work in the skyscrapered city without undergoing twice daily the grinding, grueling, time-consuming commuter trip common to most other urban areas of the United States."[13]

While BART promoters celebrated the individual's freedom to live, work, and relax in different areas in the region, they designed BART primarily to serve suburban residents who worked in the central cities. Writers spoke of the suburbs being drawn into close connection to the city. BART suburbanized the city by bringing a distinctly middle-class or suburban landscape of order and control to the city. BART described its typical rider as a suburban commuter to the city. Descriptions of BART included visions of a smoothly functioning, highly ordered, metropolitan experience. Photographs and drawings showed the trains running above or beneath city streets, a vision of a new transportation space completely removed from the chaotic city. BART stations were located near offices and downtown department stores allowing suburbanites direct access to those parts of the city they favored while allowing them to avoid the rest. The system possessed its own police force and a centralized computer system ran the trains. The system over all else exuded a sense of organization, speed, specialization, and control.[14]

Therefore, BART was sold to the public as bringing to the city a suburban landscape of order, which urban leaders embraced in hopes of reversing the economic decline in their cities. Officials also claimed the system would create "nucleated sub-centers" or smaller cities around suburban stations. Thus they promoted BART as allowing continued suburban residential growth, through the creation of job centers in the suburbs.[15]

Besides promoting its positive impact on Bay Area cities and suburbs, BART officials defended the system from criticism by stressing that it was a regional network. Oakland, Berkeley, and San Francisco city leaders all criticized BART for mismanaging the design and construction of downtown stations. The city of Berkeley sued BART over plans to build elevated tracks through its downtown. From 1963 to 1966 Berkeley city officials studied how much more it would cost to build the station and lines below ground. They undertook studies, submitted estimates, toured Toronto's rapid transit system to compare below ground alternatives, and testified before BART's board. They discovered that an underground line would cost about $12 million more than the elevated line, while BART officials claimed the additional cost would be more than $25 million. Berkeley residents then passed a bond measure to pay the additional cost. In Oakland and San Francisco, city leaders also criticized the location and aesthetics of the downtown BART stations.[16] San Francisco was especially vociferous in claiming BART's station plans failed to add to the attractiveness of the city's downtown.[17]

The *Chronicle's* architectural critic Allan Temko regularly vilified BART's engineers for their poorly designed stations and lack of concern for landscaping around the stations. He wrote an article criticizing BART's reliance on engineers to design the stations rather than architects.[18] The *Chronicle* ran a series of articles that denounced the routing of the trains through the system. One story was headlined: "Trains that Run to Wrong Places-Rapid Transit Routes Ignore Where Bay Area Riders Want to Go."[19] Critics even began equating BART with the Embarcadero Freeway debacle.[20] In August of 1966, San Francisco leaders became convinced of the need for an additional station at Davis Street. Mayor John Shelley went to Washington D.C. in a failed attempt to garner additional federal funding.[21]

Suburban leaders also criticized BART. They feared the political power of San Francisco and Oakland, particularly after BART ran into red ink. In 1966, cost overruns exceeded the $792 million bond measure and required another $150 million for completion. As a result, suburban communities feared that their stations might be reduced in size, built with fewer amenities, or even eliminated.[22]

All critics argued that BART's bureaucracy disregarded ideas from local residents. When Berkeley citizens challenged BART on undergrounding the downtown line and station, the *Chronicle* praised "Berkeley's long, valiant, determined and costly battle against the faceless BART bureaucracy."[23] The *Tribune* noted that when a regional authority "disregards the wishes of a local community, the citizens of that community are being denied the benefits of true representative government." The Berkeley case taught that it was "absolutely necessary for any community to give careful consideration to proposals" that created bodies of government outside local control.[24]

BART responded by arguing that such complaints were selfishly motivated and that BART was a regional network that could not accommodate all local desires. BART lawyer Wallace L. Kaapcke recalled that city leaders unrealistically felt there was "no reason why BART shouldn't...fix up the city while we were going through."[25] Another BART defender stated, "A pet theme of local communities is to cash in on BART by getting it to build new sewers, put in new paving and curbs, and make other improvements that they should pay for themselves."[26]

Because BART officials saw the system shaping the future of the region, one expert felt they were not concerned with local criticism.[27] BART also paid little attention to fitting into the city or suburb. Rather BART was conceived as a way to isolate travelers from the elements, especially avoiding any interaction with the dirt and crime in the city streets. BART officials believed that regional growth would adapt to the system's presence, which diminished their attention to present day realities. BART's disregard for local effects led to constant criticism from politicians and journalists, which set the stage for protests by West Oakland residents.

BLACK POLITICS AND BLACK POWER

The Black Power movement of the mid 1960s arose in response to the slow pace of economic change during the Civil Rights movement. Though the Civil Rights movement led to an end to *de jure* racial segregation, it largely failed to improve the economic plight of black America. As the Vietnam War heated up, and as self-determination struggles arose in Asian, African, and Latin American countries, black leaders began calling for urban rebellions. Leaders like Stokely Carmichael began drawing links between rebellions against American and European domination in Cuba and Vietnam and the rule by white "colonialists" in black neighborhoods within the United States. They criticized leaders like Martin Luther King, Jr., for emphasizing racial integration, and called for black pride, political power, and economic development within black neighborhoods. In the face of growing white brutality, and the killing of three civil rights workers in Selma, Alabama, in 1965, Black Power activists rejected the non-violent stance of the Civil Rights movement and insisted on the right of minorities to carry guns for self-defense against racist police. They embraced Islam, black nationalism, and the right of blacks to run their own communities. By the mid 1960s, shouts of "Black Power!" replaced the singing of "We shall overcome."[28]

The Black Power movement inspired the Black Panthers, a West Oakland based group, which rose in 1966. West Oakland is one of Oakland's oldest and poorest areas. In the nineteenth century, Portuguese, Slavs, Greeks, Spaniards, Irish, and Italians made West Oakland home.[29] Blacks who worked as railroad porters settled there in the 1860s and 1870s.[30] Black soldiers who served in the Philippines during the Spanish-American War settled in Oakland after the war. Other blacks moved to West Oakland from San Francisco following the 1906 earthquake.[31] Though they often faced discrimination, Oakland and the Bay Area had a much better racial climate and many more economic opportunities than did the South.[32]

West Oakland's black population increased during World War I as newcomers arrived and went to work in nearby shipyards, hospitals, and military bases. Many also worked at nearby box, can, bottle companies, and canneries. During World War II, good paying defense jobs in the shipyards attracted many blacks from the South to the area. Oakland's black population increased from 8,462 in 1940 to 37,327 in 1945. After the war, West Oakland contained a diverse population, which included Europeans, Asians, Hispanics, and a thriving commercial district.[33]

As whites left for the suburbs in the 1950s, West Oakland became a major black neighborhood, though its affordable housing and proximity to employers attracted poor whites, Asians, and Mexicans as well. After World War II, West Oakland residents found jobs at the Port of Oakland, the Oakland International Airport, the Alameda Naval Base, and the Oakland Naval Supply Depot, as well as at local hotels, bars, and restaurants.[34] West Oakland's population by 1966 reached 41,660, of whom 78 percent were black, 21 percent white, and 4 percent Hispanic. Forty-six percent lived below the poverty level and 75 percent were renters; 33 percent were wholly or partly on welfare and 70 percent did not own a car.[35]

The economic decline of West Oakland followed the movement of employers out of Oakland to the suburbs. Between 1950-1960, Oakland lost over 9,000 manufacturing jobs. General Motors relocated an automobile factory to Fremont in southern Alameda County. Other companies that left Oakland included General Electric Lamps Division and the Nordstrom Valve Co. Between 1960 and 1966, more than 3,000 jobs left the city.[36] While one-half of Oakland was ill housed and ill fed, the situation in the flatlands was most dire. In 1966, about 30 percent of the flatlands population was unemployed or underemployed. Of those, 60 percent were African American and 8 percent were Mexican American.

After 1960, several downtown Oakland department stores closed and the population in nearby residential areas declined precipitously.[37] Oakland downtown leaders attempted to revive the central business district by building middle-class housing in West Oakland. In 1960, Oakland contained 141,537 houses and apartments. In 1966, that figure reached 146,700. Yet that small increase belied the fact that many units had been razed. Out of 8,000 razed units, 6,000 had housed low-income residents. The 13,000 newly built units housed moderate-income groups.[38] As a result, the housing available for low-income residents became even more crowded.

In the mid 1960s, BART's transbay tube, tracks, and a station displaced hundreds of West Oakland residents. BART was only the most recent in a series of large projects that officials placed in West Oakland. The Nimitz Freeway built in 1957 had displaced West Oaklanders as had the construction of the Acorn housing projects and a large Post Office facility in the 1950s and 1960s. BART was the last straw for many residents.

These harsh realities in the mid 1960s facilitated the rise of the Black Panthers. Mainly young black men and women, the Panthers, founded in October of 1966, made national headlines by toting firearms and demanding political control of their neighborhoods. Unlike the mainstream civil rights leadership, they rejected non-violence in favor of self-defense. They fought against police brutality by patrolling West Oakland and supervising the city's officers. While their image of young black men in leather coats toting guns received much publicity, they also organized food and shoe drives, got volunteers to offer the poor legal assistance, medical care, and held educational classes for black children.[39]

Though they rejected integration, the Panthers also rejected total separatism and worked with progressive whites, particularly communists, who appeared at rallies alongside Panther leaders. The history of white activism, including the Bay Area labor movement and the free speech and anti-war movements, contributed to a somewhat integrated Black Power movement in Oakland. While the Panthers supported the quest for black cultural, economic, and political autonomy, they worked with white radicals to achieve their goals.[40] One reason for their openness to assistance from any progressive allies was their strong identification with West Oakland, which was a diverse community. To understand why West Oakland was such a center of political activity in the mid 1960s we need to look at the battle over the construction of BART through West Oakland.

The Panthers were involved in the movement against BART. In 1966, Elijah Turner wrote about watching the police arrive at a black house to enforce BART's eviction of seven elderly black women. Turner noted that too often he had witnessed whites evicting blacks and he urged the black community to take a stand against the white domination and forced removal. "How long will we continue to let this happen?" he asked.[41]

WEST OAKLANDERS CONFRONT BART

Black activists mobilized the community against BART by convincing West Oaklanders of their common interests and history. While BART officials advocated a regional identity based on consumer choice, materialism, and suburban residence, black activists emphasized that loyalty to West Oakland unified local residents across color or class divisions.

The West Oakland community mobilized around opposition to BART beginning in September of 1965 and continued through 1967. Just as Oakland, San Francisco, and Berkeley officials stood up for the interests of their cities, West Oakland activists lobbied for their community's interests as well.

In seeking to garner united community action against BART, local leaders presented West Oakland as a special place. The authors of *Habits of the Heart* contend that any united group requires the creation of "communities of memory," which involves the telling of stories about history. These stories familiarize the group with the important figures and events that communicated the values of the community.[42] West Oakland leaders forged a community of memory by founding a neighborhood biweekly newspaper called *The Flatlands*. The newspaper's title referred to the bayside location of the predominantly working-class population in Oakland and Richmond, including West Oakland. They used the term "flatlands" as a shorthand for the working class and industrial areas in contrast to the "hills," where the upper and middle classes lived in houses overlooking the Bay.[43]

The newspaper included biographies of West Oakland residents, which revealed their common experiences as southern migrants who fled discrimination and poverty to settle in West Oakland. These biographies underscored that blacks and other working-class residents had chosen to live permanently in West Oakland, buy a house, and raise a family. By presenting these biographies, the paper fought the notion disseminated by BART and others that West Oakland was simply a "ghetto" and that its residents would be better off elsewhere. By presenting West Oakland as a community with a past, the paper and West Oakland activists fought the idea that mobility was beneficial and necessary to poor people.

Activists celebrated the community's former diversity and economic vitality before new freeways destroyed housing and spurred an exodus to the suburbs. For example, Geena Ward recalled being one of the few black residents in the area in the 1940s, when West Oakland was composed of many Czechoslovaks, Puerto Ricans, and Mexicans. She spoke fondly of such diversity as a "golden age" and sadly recalled how the area had since declined economically. "We had grocery stores right there on the corner," she remembered. "It was pretty well built up." She recalled that West Oakland in those days had a movie theater and a recreation center, both long gone. Born in Nacodoches, Texas, where her father had been a sharecropper, Ward had migrated with her family to Oklahoma, and then to Los Angeles where she met her husband, who later died in a work related accident. She joined relatives in Oakland in 1940 and worked in a nearby cannery. She took in boarders to save money and finally was able to buy a house in West Oakland in the late 1950s.[44]

Similarly, Annie Richey, described as "an active resident of her neighborhood since 1945," grew up in Arkansas. Her grandparents had been slaves and she left home at the age of 16. "I was grown then, wanted to go out for myself." She worked as a migrant laborer and domestic and settled in Long Beach near Los Angeles in 1923 when her husband died. She came to Oakland with her new husband in 1943 and two years later bought a home in West Oakland. She served as a chaplain at Park Chapel First AME Church, and registered people to vote. She was also involved in the West Oakland Home and Tenants Association.[45]

Betty Stenyard grew up in Greenville, Mississippi, and worked in the fields "ever since I was large enough to work." During World War II, she and her husband migrated to Oakland and her husband found a job in the shipyards and she worked in the Naval Hospital. She was able to buy a house in West Oakland with savings after the war.[46]

The paper represented West Oakland's ongoing diversity with a biography of Mexican American Abe Tapia. The area's low rents and jobs attracted Hispanics to West Oakland. In 1960, there were 23,729 Spanish-surnamed residents, 6.5 percent of Oakland's population. Many worked in East Bay military installations, hotels, factories, canneries, and in food service. More than half of the Mexican population resided along the shoreline of the East Bay.[47] Like blacks, Mexicans had been displaced by freeway construction and urban renewal in the 1950s and 1960s.[48]

Tapia, chair of the Mexican American Unity Council in Oakland, was from Rowe, New Mexico. He left New Mexico to join the army, worked as a bomb demolition expert in Germany and France, and also served during the Korean War. He left the army in 1955 and went to Los Angeles where he stayed with cousins and worked as a welder. He then joined a brother living in Oakland and went to work for Marchant Calculators and later the United States Post Office.[49] Tapia recalled discrimination on military bases in areas where Mexicans were traditionally mistreated. "Oklahoma and Texas are the worst as far as being anti-Mexican," he noted. But the military did not segregate soldiers so he often bunked with blacks. Tapia recalled being the only white person in an "all-Negro barracks" in France.[50]

Like many black newcomers, Mexicans had migrated to the area after having suffered from racial hostility and economic deprivation elsewhere. Their common determination to overcome poverty and discrimination linked blacks and Mexicans in West Oakland. Both also wanted to maintain their culture and believed they could do so in the West Oakland community. Mexican Americans "want to be left in their own culture," said Tapia. Despite the "heavy demands" to assimilate, Tapia identified with the more recent Mexican immigrants who were the poorest workers. "It's not like the Irish or the Italians where a point comes when no more come in," Tapia argued. Their common experiences as working-class migrants who were proud of their heritage linked Mexicans and blacks in West Oakland.[51]

The biographies in *Flatlands* helped formulate a West Oakland identity built around resident loyalty to the community. Residents appeared united behind the effort to maintain West Oakland as a viable community. Along with the biographies, the paper showed that BART had displaced families who had resided in the area for numerous years. The paper highlighted the experiences of black women. BART supporters argued that rapid transit would bring families together by cutting down the time husbands spent in traffic and that the suburbs were the best place to raise a family.[52] In contrast, the presence of women and families in West Oakland indicated that though the community was poor, it was still a home for many families that BART was displacing. The image of many women fighting BART suggested that as long as the residents had some control over local politics they could revive the neighborhood. However, the building of BART and freeway construction only encouraged more out-migration of both residents and jobs.[53]

GEOGRAPHY, THE BLACK MIDDLE CLASS AND BART

Besides praising long-term residents and women, activists also tried to unify West Oaklanders by criticizing those who had left the community. Professional blacks in the sixties who found well-paying jobs in Oakland city government relocated to better housing outside of West Oakland, and sometimes further out in the suburbs. Activists portrayed professional blacks who left the ghetto as blacks who preferred to associate with whites. While whites had left the central city because of deteriorating housing and the growth of the black population, Black Panther Earl Anthony said blacks who left "aspire to the socio-economic standards of white society" and "abandon the core of the city to hopefully live side by side with white people in the hills or suburbs."[54]

White city leaders often placed middle-class blacks in charge of programs that served poor minority residents. But activists noted that middle-class blacks lived outside the community "directly between the Flatlands Negro and the white power structure" where they impeded communication between poor African Americans and city leaders. Community activists argued that because the professionals no longer lived in the ghetto, they misunderstood the problems of the poor.[55] Activists assumed that the professionals only reluctantly confronted powerful whites about racism and poverty and therefore impeded social change. "The Negro from the flatlands cannot communicate with the power structure because the power won't listen to him," noted Elijah Turner. "Instead they get their Uncle Tom answers about the flatland problems from the middle class Negro."[56] Black Panther leader Huey P. Newton summed it up by telling black city politicians to "come home and stay home."[57]

Thus, black activists praised residents who stayed in West Oakland for being loyal to the community and proud of their racial heritage. But they believed that those who had left had rejected the community in favor of living with whites. The new mobility meant all had a choice in where to live. While the professional class "abandoned" West Oakland, those who remained had "chosen" to stay out of loyalty to the community.

While BART claimed West Oakland was a ghetto, West Oakland activists used home ownership to indicate the community's continued viability. West Oakland's blacks bought their homes in the 1940s.[58] Activists criticized BART for displacing urban homeowners to build a system serving suburban commuters.

Homeownership signified hard work and sacrifice. Tapia was proud of owning his home, which was the direct result of his migration from New Mexico. Tapia stated that making "it on my own" meant buying a home. He stated he earned "everything I have with no help from anybody. Everything's from my own sweat."[59]

Homeownership reflected the efforts of the poor to improve their lives by struggling for better opportunities. Purchasing and repairing a home symbolized their histories of personal struggle and a desire for stability. One West Oakland resident was a former field worker, which intensified his desire to find a home for "my old days that I would know I wouldn't be driven from place to place."[60]

Thus, homeownership also indicated that the poor had gained control over their lives, which BART disrupted. "If you would have a home paid for, and the deeds and everything, and a man comes, shoves you out, and just gives you what he wants you to have—you wouldn't feel good," said one West Oaklander.[61]

By emphasizing the importance of homeownership, activists also argued that though the community had paid much in taxes, the neighborhood had seen few benefits. As taxpayers, West Oaklanders "have not cost our city a great deal," said a resident. "We have not had good lights for our streets, or good paved sidewalks to walk on. We have not had good sanitation. The police service has been poor."[62] Thus, the degradation of the area resulted from municipal policies which ignored the community's needs, in favor of such amenities as a new stadium, arena, and a new museum.[63]

The articles indicated that West Oakland's recent degradation was reversible given the presence of loyal West Oaklanders who had made a commitment to the area. Blacks and Mexicans praised the community's diverse history. They argued that the city had failed to maintain West Oakland by promoting the decentralization of jobs and by building structures that disrupted its residential character, including a large postal distribution center and low-income housing projects. The decline of economic vitality, the lack of jobs, and the city's general reluctance to invest in improving the area's appearance eroded its attractiveness. "People went to moving away," noted Geena Ward. "People stopped fixing up their homes. Weren't no use to change things cause sooner or later they would tell us they'd come and tear it down."[64]

West Oakland residents did not ignore the many problems in their community including crime and unemployment.   But they blamed absentee landlords and others they called "new elements" for many of the problems.[65] They also blamed city politicians for not providing adequate social services which contributed to neighborhood deterioration.[66]

JOBART AND AFFIRMATIVE ACTION

Asserting the presence of a viable community in West Oakland was part of the effort to gain more concessions from BART. But they also formed a new political organization. Faced with growing unemployment and unable to influence an insensitive bureaucracy, community leaders formed JOBART in early 1965. JOBART stood for either Justice on BART or Jobs on BART.[67] JOBART was a loosely structured coalition of two dozen civil rights organizations, church groups, and neighborhood associations. It included clergy from local churches, community leaders, political activists, and local residents. The Reverend J. Russell Brown of the First African Methodist Episcopal Church in Oakland and Reverend Alexander S. Jackson of the Church by the Side of the Road headed the organization.[68] JOBART criticized BART for hiring too few minority workers, granting few construction contracts to minority firms, and paying low prices for the homes of the displaced West Oakland residents, as well as failing to pay moving expenses.[69]

JOBART staged protests that expressed the concerns of West Oaklanders about the few minorities BART employed in the construction of the system, the low prices BART paid for houses it razed, and the lack of money for moving expenses. In 1966, only 4 of 160 BART workers were black.[70] When this was pointed out, BART blamed discrimination within construction unions. BART had signed a "no strike" agreement with the AFL-CIO building trades and teamsters, which required that BART employ only unionized workers.[71] BART claimed the union was failing to get minorities into apprenticeship programs.

JOBART argued BART should pressure the unions to hire workers residing within San Francisco, Alameda, and Contra Costa Counties whose residents funded BART. They also demanded that construction unions upgrade minority workers in lower classifications and provide on-the-job training and bilingual instruction as needed. They demanded that trainees receive full union membership and that BART's contracting employers and unions keep records on minority group employment and make the statistics available to the public.[72]

JOBART also criticized BART's eviction policies, which exacerbated numerous problems in West Oakland. JOBART asserted that those evicted had nowhere else to go because they could not afford to pay higher rents or mortgages and because whites excluded blacks from the better residential areas. "If you have a large family, if you're Negro, or Mexican-American, or Indian or Chicano or Japanese or Filipino you will be prevented from living in certain parts of the 'All-American City,'" said one resident.[73]

JOBART also demanded that BART pay fair prices for West Oakland homes that it purchased through eminent domain. Without adequate payment it was impossible for those evicted to buy new homes. One commentator noted that "BART feels that the property owners should not expect very much money for their property because their neighborhood is run down."[74] Residents deemed this unfair, given that the homeowners had not caused community decline.[75]

To garner support from inside and outside the community, JOBART held a mass meeting in February of 1966 at McClymonds High School in West Oakland. Attended by more than 300 black and Mexican American residents, the meeting featured 30 ministers who represented JOBART. The organization threatened to launch a campaign to defeat the bond issue funding the system unless BART addressed the employment and eviction issues.[76] In March of 1966, JOBART staged a public protest outside BART headquarters in San Francisco. During the protest the reverends Brown and Jackson testified before the BART directors. About 50 demonstrators marched with picket signs, which read "negotiate with JOBART," and sang civil rights songs.[77] JOBART staged another protest in April attended by 100 protestors. At that meeting, Elijah Turner of the civil rights organization CORE (Congress of Racial Equality) spoke out against union discrimination and demanded that BART require contractors to hire minority workers.[78]

These rallies garnered publicity for JOBART from the mainstream press and support for its demands from influential white leaders, many of whom were already angry with BART. JOBART supporters included the Oakland Council of Churches, local rabbis, and John S. Commins, the chancellor of the Catholic Diocese of Oakland.[79] Mayor John H. Reading of Oakland wrote a "strongly worded" letter urging BART to increase minority employment, and he endorsed "in principle" JOBART demands for more compensation for houses it purchased. The California Fair Employment Practices Commission and the United States Civil Rights Commission also criticized BART for its hiring policies.[80]

The protests and the pressure applied by white power brokers brought BART to the negotiating table. BART and JOBART officials met on March 25, 1966, at the San Francisco BART headquarters. A second meeting was held at the First AME Church in Oakland on March 31. Following these meetings, BART officials promised to place a moratorium on evictions until those displaced could find adequate housing alternatives and vowed to increase pressure on unions to hire more minorities.[81] Yet these promises did not guarantee increased employment, so JOBART continued its pressure tactics on June 5, 1966, by staging a march from the First AME Church to Lakeside Park (Photo 3). The demonstration drew about 1,000 and included the McClymonds High School Drum Corps and a number of church officials, neighborhood activists, and CORE representatives. Speakers demanded that BART increase compensation for the displaced and hire more minority workers.[82] Two days later, Mayor Reading called on BART to produce a fair hiring policy.[83]

Despite these efforts, BART was constructed as planned through West Oakland and JOBART was only partly successful in its job demands. Unlike the anti-freeway movement in San Francisco, rapid transit proved more difficult to affect for several reasons. First, unlike the freeway opponents, black activists did not receive any support from environmentalists and preservationists who favored mass transit over automobiles. Second, though white leaders stated their support of JOBART, it was understood that any changes relating to West Oakland,

Photo 3.
McClymonds High School Drum Crops Leads JOBART March. Photo from *Flatlands*, June 18-July 1, 1966.

including more money for those displaced, would cut into the money BART could spend on the downtown stations. Thus, Mayor Reading agreed only "in principle" to JOBART's request for more money for those displaced, while supporting wholeheartedly increased minority employment, which did not cost the system any more money. Oakland state assemblyman William Byron Rumford authored a bill that required that BART pay $200 per displaced family for moving expenses and $3,000 per business, but this law was not retroactive and many had already relocated by the time it went into effect.[84]

Though JOBART had little success, new federal legislation forced BART to implement an affirmative action policy.[85] Early in 1967, the U.S. Department of Housing and Urban Development (HUD) required that BART formulate a minority hiring policy in order to receive a $26 million capital grant. The money went to three contractors who awarded sub-contracts to minority-operated firms who, in turn, were required to publicize job opportunities in local junior high and high schools.[86] Yet, local activists still complained that very few blacks worked as BART apprentices or office workers. Most held low-paying positions.[87]

This legislation, moreover, did not deal with employment after the trains started running. Besides construction jobs, black leaders also demanded BART hire minorities as train operators, maintenance workers, and clerical staff. But BART faced pressure from AC Transit, the public bus system, whose workers feared that BART's opening would lead to layoffs of bus drivers. They asked BART to give former bus drivers preference after BART opened. But BART officials refused to give "exclusive preferential hiring for any specific group," either minorities or other transit workers.[88]

BART'S REGIONAL RESPONSIBILITY

BART officials argued that they had no special responsibility to provide jobs or economic development for any specific community. Yet their promotional literature celebrated the system's positive effects on the region's economy. They promised relief from traffic congestion, economic growth around stations, increased property values, and a "wider choice" of jobs, homes, and colleges.[89] When activists demanded to know how BART would benefit West Oakland, system officials produced a report called "BART and the Ghettos." The 1969 report noted the system's stations were located in minority neighborhoods, providing those who were without cars access to suburban jobs, colleges, housing, entertainment, and government offices throughout the region.[90]

But BART did not suggest it would stimulate economic development within West Oakland. Rather, its local impact would depend on how public officials utilized the system. "Precisely how well the political and economic leaders of the Bay Area will use the BART lines and stations for the benefit of blue-collar and white-collar workers alike is not a known fact. It is a matter of speculation. It can also be a matter of disillusionment if opportunities are ignored."[91] If local officials mismanaged linking BART to the present transit lines, then BART would not serve minorities as it could.

An issue more fundamental than hiring created the conflict between West Oakland residents and BART. As stated, West Oaklanders viewed their neighborhood as a tight-knit, historic community. BART argued that the system freed blacks and other poor residents from the problems of the ghetto. This conflicting view of the ghetto was a fundamental part of the antagonism between West Oakland residents and BART.

BART officials viewed the separation of home and work to be the essential feature of the modern metropolis in which different realms served specialized functions. Residents would not live in small, isolated, self-sufficient towns, but travel throughout the region. The urban riots of the 1960s were sometimes blamed on the suburbanization of jobs and the lack of minority mobility.[92]

System general manager B. R. Stokes impugned the inner city neighborhoods precisely when blacks and Mexican Americans were redefining their identities in terms of loyalty to the ghetto or barrio and demanding local economic development. "American ghettos," said Stokes, "are geographic pockets of poverty. They are also pockets of racial or social segregation." Ghetto residents "suffer acutely from almost total separation from the mainstreams of American society, from the fruits of a free enterprise economy, and from exposure to available vocational training or higher education." Stokes claimed that the ghetto residents suffered from "physical and social immobility and remoteness from jobs and job training" and were "victimized by apathy and fatalism." Stokes noted that "the non-white clearly needs mobility: for some, the freedom to move out of ghetto life on a daily basis; for others, on a lifetime basis; for all, ultimately, a choice between the two."[93]

But if BART could make suburban jobs accessible to inner city residents, why could not jobs be brought into West Oakland? Some activists proposed that BART share parking revenues with local residents, an idea BART rejected.[94] Would not greater mobility lead to increased segregation as individuals chose to associate with members of their own race and class? Stokes assumed that "psychological-social separation" was "inevitable." Rapid transit could only bring minorities to new jobs in the suburbs, not facilitate residential integration.[95] But West Oaklanders questioned why so many companies moved to the suburbs and why the poor should be forced to commute to those jobs. They saw regional mobility as the problem, not the solution.

ANTI-POVERTY PROGRAMS IN WEST OAKLAND

Simultaneously with the BART protests, there arose several controversies about who should direct anti-poverty programs in West Oakland. In 1965, the Oakland Economic Development Council (OEDC) was founded, and Oakland's white power brokers chose black professionals to manage the anti-poverty funds. Working-class West Oakland activists, however, demanded more control of local anti-poverty funds. On March 12, 1966, West Oakland residents walked out of an OEDC meeting demanding control over the board and demanding that more funds go to the poor than to the administrators of the program. West Oakland activists were adamant that black professionals should not be in charge of the programs in West Oakland. As one leader put it, "We are tired of the Uncle Toms and Aunt Jennys who listen and then carry on sweetly and do nuthin."[96] What was surprising was the level of unity amongst the West Oakland community.

In prior years, the city depended on professional blacks and moderate West Oakland homeowners to support city policies in the area.[97] But after the fight against BART, a much more unified community existed. The West Oakland Planning Council (WOPC) united over one hundred social agencies serving the poor. WOPC leaders rejected representation by black professionals who lived outside the community, and demanded their own power to determine city policy in West Oakland. Their efforts succeeded because during the BART struggle, West Oaklanders had come to have a common territorial identity that unified homeowners and tenants, whites, Mexicans and blacks. Though the BART struggle basically failed, in the long run it, along with the ongoing struggle against urban renewal and police brutality, helped gain local control of anti-poverty programs and local schools.

The battle with BART proved much more difficult because it pitted a locally mobilized community against a regional system. BART disrupted many in West Oakland and its officials rejected any responsibility. They argued that local complaints were mostly selfish and that BART's primary goal was to serve a region. The system's purpose was to make accessible jobs and services located outside the ghetto, not to finance economic improvement of West Oakland.

BART also made few concessions to city politicians. Though officials in Oakland, San Francisco, and Berkeley demanded numerous changes, only Berkeley, which paid the additional cost of putting its downtown station underground, achieved its goal. BART officials presented themselves as the defenders of regional interests against local special interests. Any changes, they claimed, added significantly to costs, benefiting local communities at the region's expense.

The legacy of the 1960s was revealed following the 1989 Loma Prieta earthquake, which destroyed the double-decked elevated freeway built through West Oakland in 1957. The California Department of Transportation immediately proposed rebuilding the structure at its original location down the middle of Cypress Avenue, a main thoroughfare in West Oakland. Environmentalists and urbanists joined West Oakland residents in forming the Citizens' Emergency Response Team (CERT) to block the reconstruction of the freeway along its original route.[98] They succeeded in forcing the state to reroute the freeway through the area devoted to railroad and port facilities. Eliminating the freeway and its noxious fumes, noise, dust, and dirt has slowly helped the revival of West Oakland as a residential/commercial area. The Cypress structure organizing effort is an example of how the poor often must use transportation issues to address other problems pertaining to jobs, housing, and schools. It also suggests that freeways are easier to block than mass transit systems.

CONCLUSION

In the mid 1960s, West Oakland residents and BART officials clashed over the impact of metropolitan mobility. BART supporters argued that regional mobility benefited all Bay Area residents. By avoiding traffic jams, BART provided consumers greater freedom of movement and more choices in housing, employment, and entertainment. BART was also touted for limiting sprawl by encouraging new development around its suburban stations.[99]

Black activists, conversely, challenged BART's positive assessment of regional mobility by pointing to the decline of West Oakland since the advent of freeways. The biographies in *Flatlands* provided a history of West Oakland as a vital community. The biographies demonstrated that many residents had chosen to live in West Oakland and would remain if they could. BART would not free them to leave; it would further undermine their neighborhood. West Oakland was not simply a ghetto and BART had an obligation to compensate residents by paying relocation costs and providing jobs.

Thus, in the context of BART, affirmative action became a form of compensation for the suburbanization of employment and for residential displacement. BART was obligated to provide jobs that would help maintain West Oakland as a viable working-class neighborhood. BART administrators claimed that the system helped blacks and so they were not obligated to implement an affirmative action program. Only after the federal government mandated a program did they implement one.[100]

Paul D. Moreno shows that two types of policies exist to eradicate job discrimination. The "disparate impact theory of discrimination" assumes that any large statistical discrepancy between minority and non-minority employment rates is inherently racist and must be attacked with policies that produce minority employment proportional to group size in the general population. The other, the "disparate treatment theory," is color blind, and compensates only individuals who personally experience discrimination.[101]   Blacks argued for both forms of compensation for West Oaklanders.   They maintained that BART harmed their community and should compensate that community with relocation payments and employment.   While that would help individuals, the community shared the benefits of such compensation which was necessary for the neighborhood to remain functional.   Since BART assisted the relocation of companies to the suburbs, it had an obligation to help maintain not just individuals but West Oakland as a viable residential community.   Thus, affirmative action served as compensation for the individuals and the community facing discriminatory treatment in the form of the politicized decision to run BART through West Oakland.

The fundamental disagreement on the value of community and mobility between BART and West Oakland resulted from the suburbanization of cities after World War II.   As suburbs succeeded in attracting jobs and residents, urban leaders looked to reverse the trend by making cities more accessible to suburbanites and by redesigning cities to make suburbanites more comfortable in the cities.   BART embodied the suburbanization process.   It brought suburban culture into San Francisco and Oakland, both in the form of middle-class white residents who commuted each day from the suburbs and in the presentment of a rapid transit experience, in the location, form, and appearance of its trains, stations, and tunnels, that appealed to suburbanites.   Its upscale trains featured plush seats and carpeting, and BART in San Francisco and Oakland linked up with office buildings and shopping malls.   Finally, by suggesting that blacks and other urbanites take BART to the suburban jobs, city residents were turned into commuters.

While freeways and rapid transit suburbanized cities, they also urbanized suburbs.   This process of the urbanization of the suburbs also created social movements as suburban residents divided over the transformation of their communities into cities. We turn to the suburban case in the following chapters in part two.

NOTES

1.   Bay Area Transportation Study Commission, *Urban Transportation Finance Report, Supplement II* (Berkeley, 1969).
2.   Social Science Research and Development Corporation, *Economic Development of Mexican-Americans: An Analysis and a Proposal* (Berkeley, 1966), 54.
3.   Donald W. Meinig, "Symbolic Landscapes: Some Idealizations of American Communities," in Meinig, ed., *The Interpretation of Ordinary Landscapes* (New York,

1979), 182; David Brodsly, *L.A. Freeway: An Appreciative Essay* (Berkeley, 1981), 33.

4.   Quoted in Howell Raines, *My Soul is Rested: Movement Days in the Deep South Remembered* (New York, 1983), 47.

5.   Kingsley Davis and Eleanor Langlois, "Future Demographic Growth in the San Francisco Bay Area," in Stanley Scott, ed., *The San Francisco Bay Area: Its Problems and Future* (Berkeley, 1966), 7.

6.   Sy Adler, "Why BART and no LART? The Political Economy of Rail Rapid Transit Planning in the Los Angeles and San Francisco Metropolitan Areas," *Planning Perspectives* 2 (1987): 161–169.

7.   David W. Jones, "California's Freeway Era in Historical Perspective," (research report, Institute of Transportation Studies, University of California-Berkeley, 1989), 269; Adler, "Why BART but no LART?," 162.

8.   Jones, "California's Freeway Era," 277.

9.   *Hayward Daily Review*, February 27, 1948.

10.   "California Living," *San Francisco Chronicle*, December 5, 1965.

11.   Press release, June 6, 1960, Adrien Falk papers, box 8, "rapid transit," BANC.

12.   Ibid.

13.   *Fortune*, September 1970.

14.   See James Bailey, "BART: The Bay Area Takes a Billion-Dollar Ride," *Architectural Forum* 124 (June 1966): 38-60. See BART photographs and drawing in *California Highways and Public Works* 45 (July-August 1966): 36–37.

15.   Richard M. Zettel, "On Studying the Impact of Rapid Transit in the San Francisco Bay Area," in United States Highway Research Board, *Impact of the Bay Area Rapid Transit System in the San Francisco Metropolitan Region* (Washington D.C., 1970), 22–23; Bailey, "BART," 38.

16.   See *Oakland Tribune*, August 1, 1967. On BART's rejection of a station at Oakland's Jack London Square, see *Tribune*, February 12, 1965.

17.   *Chronicle*, February 10, 1965; February 15, 1965; October 10, 1965; February 17, 1965; January 20, 1967.

18.   *Chronicle*, September 30, 1966; October 3, 1966.

19.   *Chronicle*, January 29, 1966.

20.   *Chronicle*, October 10, 1965.

21.   *Chronicle*, August 26, 27, 1966; June 22, 23, 29, 1967; July 21, 1967.

22.   *Chronicle*, July 28, 1967.

23.   *Chronicle*, August 1, 1966.

24.   *Tribune*, October 6, 1966.

25.   Wallace Letcher Kaapcke, "'General Civil Practice': A Varied and Exciting Life at Pillsbury, Madison & Sutro" (transcript of interview conducted 1986-1987 by Carole Hicke, Regional Oral History Office, University of California-Berkeley, p. 175.

26.   Bailey, "BART," 58.

27.   Stephen Zwerling, *Mass Transit and the Politics of Technology: A Study of BART and the San Francisco Bay Area* (New York, 1974), 79.

28.   On the Black Power movement, see William L. Van Deburg, *New Day in Babylon: The Black Power Movement and American Culture, 1965-1975* (Chicago, 1992); Hugh Pearson, *The Shadow of the Panther: Huey Newton and the Price of Black Power in America* (Reading, 1994); John T. McCartney, *Black Power Ideologies: An Essay in African-American Political Thought* (Philadelphia, 1992); Claybourne Carson, *In Struggle: SNCC and the Black Awakening of the 1960s* (Cambridge, 1981).

29.   Lee Hildebrand, "West Side Story," *East Bay Express*, September 28, 1979; *San Francisco Bay Guardian*, June 30, 1993; Beth Bagwell, *Oakland: The Story of a City* (Oakland, 1982), 90.

30.   Donald Hausler, "The Cypress Structure and the West Oakland Black Community," *From the Archives* (Winter 1990): 2; Bagwell, *Oakland*, 83.

31.   Edward Everett France, "Some Aspects of the Migration of the Negro to the San Francisco Bay Area Since 1940" (Ph.D. dissertation, University of California-Berkeley, 1962), 14.

32.   Shirley Ann Moore, "The Black Community in Richmond, California, 1910-1963, (Ph.D. dissertation, University of California-Berkeley, 1989), 206.

33.   See Charles Wollenberg, *Golden Gate Metropolis: Perspectives on Bay Area History* (Berkeley, 1985); Marilynn S. Johnson, *The Second Gold Rush: Oakland and the East Bay in World War II* (Berkeley, 1993); Douglas H. Daniels, *Pioneer Urbanites: A Social and Cultural History of Black San Francisco* (Philadelphia, 1980); Albert S. Broussard, *Black San Francisco: The Struggle for Racial Equality in the West, 1900-1954* (Lawrence, 1993).

34.   Hausler, "The Cypress Structure," 1–3.

35.   Gene Bernardi, *Income Needs in West Oakland* (Oakland, 1966), 1; Gene Bernardi, *Socio-Demographic Data on Neighborhood Family Services' Clientele* (Oakland, 1966), 20.

36.   Oakland, California, Department of Planning, *Application for Planning Grant Model Cities Program City of Oakland* (Oakland, 1967), 26; Edward C. Hayes, *Power Structure and Urban Policy: Who Rules in Oakland?* (New York, 1971), 47, 56–57.

37.   Carole Joy Abrew, "Patterns and Process of Change in Oakland, California" (master's thesis, San Francisco State University, 1973), 48, 67.

38.   *Flatlands*, March 26, 1966; Judith V. May, "Two Model Cities: Negotiations in Oakland," *Politics and Society* 2 (Fall 1971): 61.

39.   Van Deburg, *New Day in Babylon*, 160.

40.   McCartney, *Black Power Ideologies*, 145; Carson, *In Struggle*, 280.

41.   See *Black Panther*, June 20, 1967.

42.   Robert N. Bellah et al., *Habits of the Heart: Individualism and Commitment in American Life* (Berkeley, 1985), 153; Iwona Irwin-Zarecka, *Frames of Remembrance: The Dynamics of Collective Memory* (New Brunswick, 1994), 47–65.

43.   An incomplete run of the *Flatlands* is available at the Oakland History Room, main branch, Oakland Public Library.

44.   *Flatlands*, May 21-June 4, 1966.

45.   *Flatlands*, August 13-August 27, 1966.

46.   *Flatlands*, November 18-December 2, 1966.

47.   Gene Barnardi, *Characteristics of the Spanish Surname Population in the City of Oakland* (Oakland, California,1966), 2.

48.   Milton E. Ortega, *A Critical Analysis of the Spanish Surname Population of Oakland, California* (Oakland, 1968), 7.

49.   *Flatlands*, April 23-May 6, 1966.

50.   *Flatlands*.

51.   Ibid.

52.   *Chronicle*, January 23, 1966.

53.   For a discussion of the problem of growing numbers of jobs in the suburbs and their inaccessibility to minority workers residing in the central cities, see "Exploring Spatial Mismatch--A Symposium," *Professional Geographer* 48 (November 1996): 417–67.

54.   *Black Panther*, June 20, 1967.

55.   *Flatlands*, Saturday, April 9, 1966.

56.   Ibid.

57.   Ibid., May 15, 1967. See also Huey P. Newton, *Revolutionary Suicide* (New York, 1973), 14–43.

58.   Daniels, *Pioneer Urbanites*, 164.

59.   *Flatlands*, April 23-May 6, 1966.

60.   *Flatlands*, August 13-August 27, 1966.

61.   *Flatlands*, March 12, 1966.

62.   Ibid.

63. May, "Two Model Cities," 61.
64. *Flatlands*, May 21-June 4, 1966.
65. *Flatlands*, March 12, 1966.
66. *Flatlands*, May 21-June 4, 1966.
67. This ambiguity in JOBART's name reflects a central point. Blacks criticized BART planners for running the system through West Oakland, yet they also called for jobs on the system. The imprecise name expressed well these two conflicting notions about the community's goals.
68. *Chronicle*, February 10, 1966.
69. On JOBART, see Gene Barnardi, *Evaluation Analysis of the Council of Social Planning's Neighborhood Organization Program* (Oakland, 1966); Patrick J. Mahoney, *Minority Employment in the Construction of BART* (n.p., 1966); Amory Bradford, *Oakland's Not for Burning* (New York, 1968), 51; Ralph M. Kramer, *Participation of the Poor* (Englewood Cliffs, 1969), 146–147.
70. *Chronicle*, March 11, 1966.
71. Mahoney, *Minority Employment*, 23.
72. Ibid., 1.
73. *Flatlands*, March 26, 1966.
74. *Flatlands*, March 12, 1966.
75. Ibid.
76. *Chronicle*, February 8, 1966; *Tribune*, February 10, 1966; Bradford, *Oakland's Not for Burning*, 51.
77. *Chronicle*, March 11, 1966.
78. *Chronicle*, April 29, 1966.
79. *Chronicle*, November 30, 1965.
80. *Tribune*, May 27, 1966; June 7, 1966; June 10, 1966.
81. *Flatlands*, April 9, 1966.
82. *Tribune*, June 5, 1966.
83. Mayor Reading also accused the construction unions of discrimination. See *Tribune*, January 5, 1967.
84. *California Voice*, July 8, 1966.
85. *Chronicle*, January 13, 1967.
86. *Chronicle*, July 21, 1967.
87. *Chronicle*, July 28, 1967; May 31 1968.
88. Bay Area Rapid Transit District, Minutes, February 8, 1968.
89. San Francisco Bay Area Rapid Transit District, *San Francisco Bay Area Rapid Transit: An Investment in the Future* (San Francisco, 1967).
90. "BART and the Ghettos," *Rapid Transit* 11:3 (Summer 1969), 1–4.
91. Ibid.
92. Jones, "California's Freeway Era," 246.
93. "BART and the Ghettos," 1–4.
94. *Tribune*, March 12, 1966.
95. Ibid.
96. David Kirp, *Just Schools: The Idea of Racial Inequality in American Schools* (Berkeley, 1982), 235; May, "Two Model Cities, 63–65.
97. Hayes, *Power Structure and Urban Policy*, 122–123.
98. Hausler, "The Cypress Structure," 3.
99. Dennis Dingemans, *Residential Subcentering and Urban Sprawl: The Location of Higher-Density, Owner-Occupied Housing Around the Concord Line BART Stations* (Berkeley, 1975).
100. San Francisco Bay Area Rapid Transit District, *Minutes*, February 8, 1968.
101. Paul D. Moreno, *From Direct Action to Affirmative Action: Fair Employment Law and Policy in America, 1933-1972* (Baton Rouge, 1997), 1.

PART TWO

---·×·---

SUBURB INTO CITY

3

MULTICULTURAL HISTORY
IN SAN JOSE

On June 1, 1969, an estimated 75,000 spectators lined the streets of downtown San Jose to witness the revival of the city's Grand Floral Parade, the culmination of the week-long "Fiesta de las Rosas" marking the 200th anniversary of the first Spanish mission in California. The celebration featured a golf tournament, a grand ball, a rodeo, and a long-horn steer drive through downtown. Lorne Greene, who played "Ben Cartwright" on the television series *Bonanza*, served as grand marshall. The crowd enjoyed the colorful procession of high school marching bands, drill teams, drum and bugle corps, antique cars, mounted horsemen, and flower-covered floats.[1]

The order of the parade, however, soon dissolved as 75 to 100 Chicano youths, wearing black berets, amassed on both sides of First Street carrying placards denouncing the fiesta. The protestors entered the parade and marched along with the other participants. After uniformed and plain-clothed police officers blocked their way, a melee ensued (Photo 4). The officers beat demonstrators with night sticks and made 30 arrests. At least a dozen Chicanos and three police officers suffered serious injuries that required hospitalization.[2]

Recounting the incident, the *San Jose Mercury-News* repeatedly called the protestors "Chicano militants." The paper's reporter quoted a police officer who accused the Chicanos of inciting the riot by throwing fire-crackers, rocks, and bottles at parade participants.[3] But Jorge Acevedo of the Chicano Confederación of Santa Clara County said the protest was peaceful until the police attacked the demonstrators without warning.[4] The police accused the Chicanos of using walkie-talkies and bullhorns to direct the "well organized" riot. The police blamed "black beret militant Anselmo (Sal) Candelaria, 25, one of the apparent ringleaders of the violence" who ran "in the street riling up his followers, and screaming and shouting in incoherent English and Spanish." The police arrested Candelaria and took him to Andrews State Hospital, a mental facility, rather than the county jail. "He was not acting like a sane man, so we committed him," reasoned a police officer afterward.[5]

The Chicanos recalled the event very differently. They had planned to demonstrate peacefully against the inclusion in the parade of a rancher on horseback driving a Mexican "peon" walking behind a burro. The Chicanos insisted that the police "waded in among women, children, and priests, turning a peaceful demonstration into a bloody turmoil."[6] Chicanos accused undercover police of infiltrating their organizations in order to set up the attack.[7] In the days leading up to the event, a local paper stated that the Chicanos had vowed to "halt" the parade, increasing tensions and making the police quick to overreact to any disturbance.[8]

Understanding the riot requires that we look at San Jose's history and

Photo 4:
Chicanos Clash with Police at Fiesta De Las Rosas, Downtown San Jose, 1969.

Photo courtesy of Richard Diaz.

growth into a major city after World War II. The fiesta stemmed from the attempt by business leaders and politicians to stimulate San Jose's downtown economy, which had declined in the 1950s due to competition from outlying shopping malls. We have seen how attempts to suburbanize downtown San Francisco and Oakland to attract outsiders stimulated a backlash from local residents. Similarly, the confrontation over the fiesta resulted from opposition by Chicanos to elite attempts to urbanize downtown San Jose.

After World War II, new highways, interstate trucking, and lower tax rates spurred residential and industrial expansion in the suburbs. Besides new factories, the suburbs attracted finance, insurance, banking, electronic, and service industries. With an increased number of affluent workers, suburbs invested in art and cultural centers, amenities that cities previously monopolized. This is not to say suburbs became cities. Most suburbs remained much more homogeneous than cities, though that was changing with the influx of many African, Latino, and Asian Americans.[9] Suburban leaders attempted to bring urban cosmopolitanism to suburban downtowns in order to reflect the prosperity of their increasingly autonomous communities and to increase community pride and support for investment in new development.

By the mid 1960s, a growing Mexican American and Asian population

Figure 4.
Downtown San Jose and Mexican Neighborhoods, 1970.

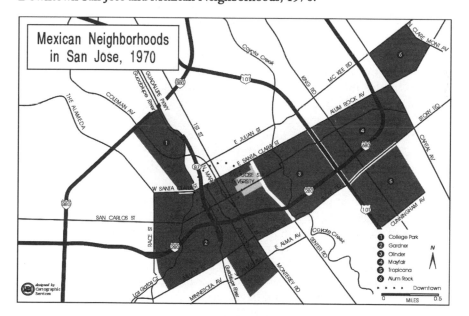

made San Jose quite diverse. Many poor Mexicans settled in the older residential areas around downtown where cheap housing predominated. The eastside barrios in the Mayfair district were especially notorious (Figure 4). The area was known as *Sal Si Puedes*, "Get out if you can." City officials feared further encroachment by the growing barrios, and they also believed that San Jose's downtown inadequately expressed its metropolitan importance. Rather than a vibrant city, San Jose was portrayed nationally and locally as a large suburb, one of many suburbs covering the South Bay's once lush farmland. By the mid 1960s, city leaders hoped to redevelop downtown into an urban center. But their attempt to use history to get community support for downtown investment produced a sharp conflict about San Jose's past.

HISTORY AND MULTICULTURALISM

The presentation of American history has become increasingly contentious since the 1960s. Both the left and the right criticize American history textbooks over the issue of multiculturalism. On the one hand, conservatives claim that new history textbooks downplay or ignore entirely the important contributions of the so-called "dead white males," prominent politicians, inventors, scientists, and military heroes, and pay too much attention to the struggles by immigrants, workers, women, and minorities against racism, sexism, and economic exploitation. Conservatives also claim that the revisionist texts ignore the influence of religion in shaping the values of the nation and of its historical leaders. Rather than producing objective history, these books, the critics claim, distort the past in order to undermine national pride and divide the nation into grievance groups that demand special consideration for the wrongs of the past.[10] On the other hand, supporters of multiculturalism criticize the textbooks for excluding ethnic groups or for slighting the history and culture of minority or immigrant populations.[11]

History has always been used to promote various political and social agendas.[12] It's been said that history is written by the victors, and all nations present their own history in the most favorable light possible. But prior to the 1960s, white males had generally free reign over the production of American history textbooks. Some women, workers, and ethnic groups wrote their own versions of the past, which did not gain widespread readership.[13] In the 1960s, the Civil Rights movement encouraged minorities to write their own histories and to insist that historians include their perspectives in high school and college textbooks.

Also, during the 1950s and 1960s historians began turning away from the study of elite Americans and began researching and writing about the lives of ordinary Americans, including immigrants, minorities, and women, in what came to be called the "new social history." Since most ordinary Americans faced poverty, experienced labor exploitation, racism, and sexism, the new studies concentrated on those unfortunate realities of the nation's past. By showing how working men and women struggled against the forces of inequality by joining labor unions, women's organizations, and ethnic-based social, economic, and political associations, these histories helped increase group identification and pride.[14]

But critics of multicultural history, like Arthur M. Schlesinger, Jr., maintain that the emphasis on minority history distorted the past. In *The Disuniting of America*, Schlesinger denounces multiculturalism as history written to make groups feel good about themselves rather than to represent the past accurately.[15] Schlesinger describes and then vilifies the most extreme examples of Afrocentric history, making the work appear petty, selfish, and delusional. Schlesinger fails to discuss the reasons why individuals become so concerned about writing and studying the history of their ethnic or racial group. In fact, who writes history can determine who holds power. Writing their own history is not merely "therapeutic" but determines very real issues such as control of the redevelopment of urban and suburban space.[16]

This chapter analyzes the struggle in San Jose over the celebration of local history in the late 1960s. Chicano activists clashed with middle-class Mexican American and Anglo civic boosters over local history, Mexican American identity, and urban redevelopment. Chicanos criticized middle-class Anglos and Mexican Americans for producing a Chicano history that, they argued, obscured their group's ongoing struggle against racism and poverty. Chicano activists also challenged city investment in downtown commercial development, which they claimed ignored the needs of poor barrio residents living near the central business district. They argued that officials needed to direct their efforts toward ending poverty rather than trying to attract conventioneers, shoppers, and other tourists into downtown San Jose. City officials were looking to lure outsiders into the city because the freeway system made San Jose accessible to residents throughout the region. The multicentered metropolis thus encouraged the Chicano movement in San Jose.

THE SUBURBANIZATION OF SAN JOSE

In the mid 1960s, San Jose faced an identity crisis. Rapid growth created general prosperity. Yet the growth took place on the edges of the city and the downtown was in decline. The downtown lacked any distinguishing features that would give it a strong national identity. Leaders started discussing how to give city residents a stronger sense of community. In their search for an identifying feature, officials turned to the city's history. San Jose originated as a Spanish pueblo in 1777. It served as a stopping-off point between Monterey and San Francisco for

Indian, mestizo (mixed bloods), and Spanish residents of the Spanish California.[17]

Subsequent settlers were attracted to the rich farmland and long growing season. Santa Clara Valley in the 1800s became a valuable location first for grain and produce farming, attracting whites and Asian farmers. In 1864, the railroad linked San Jose to San Francisco. Up through World War II, the Santa Clara Valley was a lush agricultural area where fruit and vegetable fields and canneries proliferated. By the 1950s, the Santa Clara Valley was a major producer of canned fruits and vegetables.[18]

San Jose grew rapidly in the early 1900s. Electric streetcar lines made downtown accessible to residents throughout the Santa Clara Valley. By the 1940s, downtown San Jose was the commercial heart of the valley. San Jose's growth stemmed partly from its isolation in the South Bay, which gave it a monopoly on providing services to Santa Clara Valley farmers.[19]

San Jose was at the forefront in providing municipal services. City officials erected electric street lights in the early 1890s. In 1916, San Jose was one of the first California cities to hire a city manager. San Jose leaders initiated city planning efforts, which in 1927 produced a major thoroughfare plan and in 1929 a comprehensive zoning ordinance regulating building height.[20] To mark the city's rise in status as the center of the valley in the 1890s, officials built in downtown a two-hundred-foot iron tower that supported powerful arc lights providing "a giant beacon lighting the entire length and breadth of the valley."[21]

But after World War II its urban image declined. Suburban development exploded in and around San Jose. Between 1944 and 1950, city planners approved over 490 separate subdivisions. San Jose annexed surrounding fields in anticipation of residential development. Few incorporated towns or natural barriers restricted the city's growth, unlike in San Francisco or Oakland. Moreover, its leaders supported horizontal expansion and aggressively extended the city's borders. San Jose city manager A. P. Hamann was quoted as envisioning the city as the "Los Angeles of the north."[22] The South Bay offered an attractive alternative to the higher housing costs that prevailed in San Francisco and the East Bay suburbs.

The many new industries that came to the Santa Clara Valley after the war also stimulated sprawling growth. In the 1950s, Ford and General Motors assembly plants relocated to the South Bay, bringing many new workers and their families to the area. Veterans who had shipped out from San Francisco during World War II and the Korean War returned permanently to the area attracted by good jobs, inexpensive housing, and the pleasant climate.[23]

In the 1950s, the South Bay became a center of the growing electronics

industry.   Ex-servicemen working at nearby bases provided local
connections to military contractors.   Defense research during the Cold
War led to the hiring of armament and aerospace engineers.   Electrical
engineers at Stanford University developed new computer technologies.
Ordnance employment in the valley increased from 1,300 in 1955 to
27,000 in 1963.   Electronics workers increased from 2,700 in 1949 to
34,000 in 1966.   By 1966, almost 60,000 were employed in aerospace-
related industries.   Between 1943 and 1960, over 330 new industries
located in the county, including General Electric, Sylvania, Varian,
Hewlett-Packard, Ford, IBM, and Lockheed.[24]

Many of these new engineering firms were located in South Bay
suburbs like Mountain View, Palo Alto, and Sunnyvale, and their
workforce settled in those areas and San Jose.   Rapid population growth
produced sprawling suburban developments located along new freeways.
Shopping malls proliferated and San Jose was increasingly suburban.
Between 1950 and 1960, the city expanded from 17 to 64 square miles,
while its population grew from 95,000 to 204,000. Annexation continued
during the 1960s, and by 1970 San Jose encompassed 137 square miles
and nearly 500,000 residents.[25]   City manager Hamann, in the 1950s and
1960s, directed the city's annexation of 1,377 outlying districts, an
average of more than 72 annexations per year.[26] Total population of Santa
Clara county went from 291,000 in 1950 to 883,000 in 1965.   San Jose's
population increased 66 percent during the 1960s, making it one of the
fastest growing metropolitan areas in America.   Since the boom attracted
workers from throughout the country, two-thirds of the city's population
increase was due to in-migration and only a third due to births.[27]

Thus, before World War II San Jose had a thriving commercial
district, complete with extensive streetcar links, but after the war, even as
the city prospered, San Jose's downtown lost its commercial vibrancy as
residents and businesses increasingly located outside the central business
district. The city even hurt downtown's development by moving city hall
out of downtown, removing many government workers who had
patronized downtown stores during their lunch hour.[28]   Shopping malls
provided the city with tax revenue but siphoned customers away from
downtown.   The lack of investment meant downtown stores decayed.
"By the late 1960s," a city planner noted, "the Central Business District
had become an area of under use, with rapidly deteriorating structures. It
no longer had the identity as the commercial and business focal point for
the Santa Clara Valley."[29]

Suburban growth and the declining downtown commercial area
created an identity crisis in San Jose in the 1960s. San Jose's nebulous
boundaries did not help. Planners criticized city boundaries that ran
"haphazardly over the map," confounding residents and blocking "the
development of a sense of community."[30]   Such development was labeled

"slurban" growth, and San Jose seemed the embodiment of suburban America, characterized by the proliferation of automobiles, ecological problems, garish commercial strip architecture, and the elimination of open space and agricultural land.[31] While San Jose in many ways was a typical "edge city," it was atypical in that it had once possessed a thriving downtown, which heightened the sense of downtown decline.

In the 1960s, planners concluded that despite the drawbacks of sprawl, residential and industrial growth away from downtown was the "expression of the contemporary goals and values of a greater part of the inhabitants of the city of San Jose."[32] Thus, the citizens supported a suburban lifestyle, which planners found created problems in reviving downtown to give San Jose an "identity" as a cohesive, united metropolis. Planners insisted that the downtown needed renewal "to better serve the city and the south bay." They also argued that only with an impressive downtown could San Jose be recognized as "one of the three metropolitan centers of the Bay Area urban complex."[33] The city needed to "attract and hold the interest of travelers to the core and to build their impression of the core area as a desirable destination rather than as a corridor for through travel." An exciting downtown would also encourage residents of expanding Santa Clara Valley suburbs to identify with San Jose as the center of the South Bay. If San Jose were to stop South Bay residents from driving to San Francisco and Oakland to spend their "entertainment dollar," it would have to invest in urban amenities.[34]

THE URBANIZATION OF DOWNTOWN

In the mid 1960s, concerned with the decline of downtown, city officials proposed new construction and reviving the city's La Fiesta de las Rosas parade and festival. Held from 1926 until the mid 1930s, the fiesta had featured flower-covered floats, a baby parade, museum exhibits, junior olympics, and bicycle races. Its chief purpose had been to draw residents and businesses to the Santa Clara Valley, as the Rose Parade had done in Los Angeles.[35]

The 1969 fiesta's official program made it clear that its sponsors hoped the revival of the festival would end the impression that San Jose was just a sprawling suburb that "lacked a sense of identity." The festival's revival would provide "an identifiable character for San Jose." The construction of freeways and tremendous growth had made it "difficult to talk to one another," and the fiesta would "re-establish a sense of community identity, community pride."[36] The organizers also noted that the festivities would attract "people and business activity to downtown."[37]

Photo 5.
Lorne Greene with the Fiesta Queen and Mexican Charros, 1969.

Photo courtesy of Richard Diaz.

The fiesta committee, led by Mary Jeanne Sauerwein, tabbed Lorne Greene as grand marshall (Photo 5). Greene starred in the cowboy show *Bonanza*. The "Cartwrights" were the television version of the independent settler families now moving into new suburban developments. But in the cultural upheavals of the 1960s, Native Americans, Asians, and Mexicans attacked the frontier myth by arguing that their ancestors had experienced oppression rather than opportunity in the West.

Therefore, rather than celebrating only the Anglo cowboy myth, city officials pointed to the city's multicultural past by asserting the good relations that existed between Indians and Spanish missionaries, and the role of the Spanish and Indians in settling the region and founding the pueblo at San Jose in 1777.

Originating in the late-nineteenth century in Los Angeles, the Spanish myth portrayed the Spanish missionaries as tirelessly Christianizing and "civilizing" the Native Americans. Unlike the Anglos, the myth said, the Spanish missionaries incorporated the natives into sacred and civil society.[38] This allowed Anglo city boosters to ignore the extermination of Native Americans by white Americans.

The Spanish myth became readily identifiable by its many icons such as adobe walls, churches, courtyards, red-tile roofs, and colonnades. By suggesting that white Spaniards first colonized the Southwest, establishing the forts, towns, and missions that grew into the region's largest cities, the myth excluded Mexicans from the history of the Southwest. In fact, "pobladores" who came with the Spanish missionaries were mixed raced, also called "mestizos," and included numerous Indians who migrated from Mexico. In celebrating the Spanish, Anglo city leaders ignored the history of Mexican settlers, who since the late-nineteenth century faced intense racism and segregation in the poorest sections of many cities.[39]

In 1955, the Junior Chamber of Commerce proposed reviving La Fiesta de las Rosas but not until 1966 did serious planning begin. The festival's main proponent, Mary Jeanne Sauerwein, argued that city officials had not been attentive to fostering "the cultural and aesthetic beauty" of San Jose. "We need to do something to distinguish our city and the Santa Clara Valley."[40] The fiesta revival received enthusiastic business and political support. A non-profit corporation, La Fiesta de las Rosas de San Jose, Inc., was formed. The committee requested $31,200 in city funding and hired a well-known San Jose and Los Angeles public relations man as executive director. The committee raised more than $300,000, much of it coming from San Jose businesses.

The fiesta supporters included professional Mexican-Americans. Luis G. Juárez, the San Jose community development director, urged the fiesta's revival. He was joined by numerous other prominent local Mexican Americans. Rather than fighting the Spanish myth, they felt they could use the myth, but alter it to make Anglos more aware of the Mexican involvement in the founding of San Jose. The fiesta would celebrate the Anglo, Mexican, and Spanish roles in the city's history.

Juárez was personally proud of San Jose's growth. San Jose's post-war expansion benefited Mexican Americans, like Juárez, who had become city workers in the 1950s and 1960s. These professionals were part of what some historians refer to as the "Mexican American generation," men and women who came of age just before and during World War II.[41] They included men like Edward R. Roybal, elected to the Los Angeles city council in 1949, and Raymond L. Telles, mayor of El Paso from 1957-1961. Many had served in the U.S. military and used the G.I. Bill to become the first in their families to go to college and on to professional careers. They fought discrimination by creating civil rights organizations such as the League of United Latin American Citizens (LULAC) in 1929 and the American G.I. Forum in 1948. They founded newspapers, were very patriotic, and encouraged Mexicans to learn English, naturalize, and vote. Yet they fought the segregation of Mexicans in inferior housing and schools, job discrimination, and voting rights abuses.[42] They sponsored English classes, ran candidates for political office, and worked with sympathetic whites to achieve a just society.

They concentrated their activism on eradicating the urban problems faced by Mexicans in Southwestern cities. Many in the Mexican American generation resided in Southwestern cities that during and after the war participated in the booming sunbelt economy, which required well-trained workers. The 1970 U.S. census indicated that the city of San Jose employed nearly 700 Mexican American men and 500 women as municipal workers, predominantly teachers, clerics, along with social workers, recreational leaders, and postal employees.[43] In the 1960s, San Jose Mexican Americans also worked in federal anti-poverty agencies, like the model cities and Economic Opportunity programs. Mexicans also worked in the Welfare Department, ran job training, and taught in the public schools.[44]

For Juárez, San Jose's rise after the war reflected his personal success and provided him with professional opportunities. In the 1950s, he attended the University of California at Berkeley where he earned a master's degree in social welfare in 1957. He became a San Jose restaurant inspector and represented California at a World Health Organization meeting in Mexico. In 1964, he was appointed director of community development and assistant to the city manager of San Jose on neighborhood blight. Juárez became an aid to city manager A. P. Hamann and also wrote a column on Mexican American history and culture for the *San Jose Mercury-News*.[45]

Juárez's personal success made him proud of the city but he lamented the decline in the public's knowledge of local history. He noted that several San Jose street names had been changed from Spanish to Anglo names. "There is a growing concern developing among Mexican Americans who fear that our city is losing a cherished tradition as a Spanish pueblo."[46] He urged the resumption of the Fiesta de las Rosas in order to publicize more widely the city's Spanish/Mexican heritage.

Juárez praised the Spanish past of the city. "Don Felipe de Neve, governor of California under the crown of Spain in 1777, first saw the potential of the San Jose area to be the site of California's first civil settlement. Throughout its long and eventful history, San Jose has achieved an important place in the development of the state, recently becoming California's fourth largest city. In addition to being the first Spanish pueblo, it was the state's first capital and the first incorporated city. With union and foresight, San Jose can become one of America's great cities." Juárez believed that history would distinguish San Jose from other cities and unite local residents. "Many citizens of San Jose have long sought to give our community the identity it needs to set it apart from other western cities and to generate pride and a feeling of belonging among its old and new residents."[47]

By celebrating both Spanish and Mexican heritage, Juárez embraced a panethnic identity. He and other professional Mexican Americans supported the fiesta, which they saw as linking all the cultures of Latin America and Spain. While they accepted the Spanish myth, they used it to increase knowledge of the Mexican contributions to the founding of the cities by noting the common cultural heritage of the Spanish and Mexican founders of the city.[48]

Their effort to conflate Spanish and Mexican culture into a pan-Latino identity was not new. After the Mexican War in 1848, some Mexicans identified themselves as Spanish, differentiating themselves from working-class Mexican immigrants in order to avoid Anglo hostility. In New Mexico, Hispanos saw themselves as Spanish because they did not feel as though "Mexico" was an important part of their heritage, although many could not actually trace their family history to Spain.[49]

Furthermore, to unite the diverse Spanish-speaking community, some Mexican Americans embraced a pan-Latino identity in the nineteenth century. In 1894, a Tucson mutual aid society, Alianza Hispano Americana, was founded by a Mexican and a Spaniard. The association's name suggested the need for an alliance between Mexicans and Spaniards in the Southwest.[50] In southern California, Ignacio L. López, editor of the Spanish-language newspaper *El Espectador*, celebrated both Spanish and indigenous cultures, arguing that each contributed to his Mexican heritage. He praised the community's Spanish and Indian heritage.[51] The name of the first Mexican American civil rights organization, the League of United Latin American Citizens (LULAC), was chosen precisely to encourage Latino groups to get beyond divisions over national origins. An earlier group called the League of Latin American citizens stated its intent to serve "citizens of the United States of Mexican or Spanish extraction."[52] Another civil rights organization, El Congreso, founded in 1938 by Guatemalan immigrant Luisa Moreno, encouraged the trade union movement among "Mexican and Spanish-speaking people."[53]

By the 1960s, Mexican American professionals in San Jose accepted and acknowledged the historical myth of a glorious Spanish past. Yet they did not seek to hide their Mexican origins. They did not see any conflict in celebrating the city's Spanish history as well as its Mexican heritage. They wished to include both cultures in any display of local history. "We are proud that our city was founded on Spanish and Mexican tradition and we want to preserve that tradition," said a Mexican American community leader.[54]

The Mexican American generation's acceptance and use of the Spanish myth reflected the fact that Anglo city leaders were increasingly turning to Mexican culture to attract newcomers to their city. New festivals held in the 1960s throughout the Southwest included Mexican handicrafts, music, food, and dancing. This was largely because the Mexican population was a significant and growing part of the urban population, and many had become local leaders, some gaining public office. Anglo politicians wanted the support of Mexican American voters, and Anglo merchants wooed Mexican American shoppers.[55]

For example, in San Jose, city officials launched a week-long celebration of Mexican Independence Day in September of 1966. During "Mexican Week," city officials, with the assistance of the Comisión Honorifica Mexicana, transformed the city's plaza into "another Olvera Street" with Mexican food concessions, curios, and folk music. The festivities concluded with a traditional Mexican Parade and Queen's Ball.[56]

Though they celebrated Mexican Independence Day, Mexican Americans continued to insist on assimilation by arguing against a total identification with Mexico. They expected new immigrants and other Mexicans to embrace a Latino identity. This required that newcomers distance themselves somewhat from the culture of Mexico and embrace a Latino identity that was unique to the United States. Giving up on national identities was not necessary but they called on Mexicans and other immigrants from Latin America to acknowledge also a Latino identity.

Their identification as Americans remained strong as well. In the 1966 celebration of Mexican Independence Day, San Jose Mexican Americans wanted Adolfo J. Domínguez, the Mexican consul general, to serve as the parade's grand marshall. The consul refused after learning that Ronald Reagan, who was running for governor, would also march in the festivities. Domínguez criticized the Mexican American parade sponsors for inviting the conservative politician to participate in "what is primarily a Mexican cultural affair."[57] Offended and embarrassed, Mexican American leaders castigated Domínguez for "statements he made against Reagan" and the next year they did not invite the consul general to attend the parade.[58]

By celebrating both Spanish and Mexican cultures, La Fiesta de las Rosas was a pan-Latino event. It included the idealization of Mexican folk art as superior to the products of American consumer culture, which many were questioning in the 1960s. As the official program noted, "culture and the arts have always played a significant role in the lives of Mexican people, not only as expression of their artistic talents, but also as a means of expressing the complexity of their feelings and frustrations." The fiesta featured an exhibit by the Mexican sculptor Jose S. Holguin, "a man who despite his lack of formal education captured the hearts of the

Mexican people."[59] The fiesta also included 149 lithographs depicting the history of the Mexican revolution.

Thus, the Mexican American and Anglo supporters of the fiesta believed the celebration was an inclusive event that offered positive examples of Mexican and Spanish history in San Jose. However, the event coincided with the rise of a new generation of Mexican Americans who disavowed any association with Spain and the Spanish conquest of the Southwest.

THE CHICANO GENERATION

The Chicano movement combined aspects of the Civil Rights, anti-war, and the Black Power movements. In the late 1960s, young Mexican Americans protested the Vietnam War, the exploitation of migrant farm workers, and racial discrimination in housing, employment, and education. Many were college students influenced by the third world student strikes of 1968 and 1969 at San Francisco State and at the University of California-Berkeley. Also influential were the United Farm Workers and the Black Panthers.[60] They chose the name "Chicano" to indicate their alliance with working-class Mexicans and to distinguish themselves from older Mexican Americans who they felt too willingly assimilated middle-class Anglo American values.[61]

The Chicano movement had four distinct components. In New Mexico, Reies López Tijerina formed the Alianza Federal de Mercedes (Federal Alliance of Land Grants).[62] Tijerina maintained that the state's poor tenant farmers had the right to reclaim land taken illegally by the United States after the Mexican War.[63] César Chávez formed the United Farm Workers (UFW) union in 1963 in California's Central Valley. The UFW was the first union successfully to mobilize poor migrant workers and demand that growers improve wages and working conditions.[64] Rodolfo "Corky" Gonzales organized Chicanos in the "Campaign for Justice," which sponsored Spanish language and Mexican history classes, and cultural events in Denver. Gonzales also wrote the epic poem "I am Joaquin," in which he stated that Chicanos should maintain their ethnic culture and language rather than embrace Anglo American values.[65] Finally, under the political leadership of José Angel Gutiérrez, Mexican Americans in Crystal City, Texas, gained control of the town council and school board. In 1967, he founded the Chicano political party La Raza Unida (The United Race).[66]

These separate components of the Chicano movement had several commonalities. Chicano activists endeavored to increase Mexican American ethnic pride, believing that decades of racism in the Southwest had discouraged the maintenance of traditions. Maintaining ethnic pride required reestablishing ties with Mexico and Mexican immigrants, a group that, Chicanos felt, middle-class Mexican Americans had ignored.[67] Chicanos participated in electoral politics and protested in the streets denouncing white racism, police brutality, the Vietnam War, and social inequality. Yet historian Edward J. Escobar notes that the movement was "essentially reformist, not revolutionary."[68]   Nevertheless, undercover Federal Bureau of Investigation agents infiltrated the movement and provoked clashes with police that resulted in the beating and arrest of Chicano demonstrators at protests, and the death of *Los Angeles Times* journalist Rubén Salazar.[69] Police brutality was a part of all Southwestern Mexican neighborhoods.   In San Jose, police killed a Mexican youth Robert García, on July 26, 1970, which sparked efforts in the Mexican community to organize a citizen review board.[70]

The movement included Los Angeles high school students who walked out of class protesting racist teachers and the lack of Chicano instructors. Vietnam veterans (*veteranos*) criticized the military for the war and for putting poor whites and minorities on the front lines. Chicanos organized a group called the Brown Berets (known as the Black Berets in San Jose), which patrolled barrio streets, documenting police brutality or unfair arrests, search, and seizure. Chicano/a writers, poets, and artists provided the icons necessary for creating a new community identity.   Artists   painted   murals   featuring   Aztec   images,   political commentary, and Mexican folk symbols.   The murals publicized the movement, expressed the commitment of Mexican American youth to assist barrio residents, increased ethnic pride, and asserted Chicano control over urban space.[71]

The Civil Rights movement greatly influenced the Chicano movement. Yet, just as significant for mobilizing Chicanos was the fact that Southwestern cities after World War II grew horizontally following new highways and freeways. This form of urban growth placed the Mexican community in a precarious position. In the nineteenth and early twentieth centuries, Mexicans faced racism in cities, yet the abundance of land throughout the Southwest meant new towns grew up around Chicano barrios, and Chicanos maintained a degree of autonomy within their traditional communities. Pre-World War II urban growth, based on interurban railways in Los Angeles, for example, bypassed many small Chicano settlements, leaving their residents untouched.[72] Yet after World War II, automobile-led urban expansion pushed Chicanos out of small settlements in the urban hinterland and forced them into overcrowded urban barrios, which became susceptible to urban renewal efforts in the 1960s. As Chicanos became intensely segregated in impoverished barrios, they bore the brunt of stereotyping and became associated with urban decline.[73]

During the 1960s, California's Mexican population doubled as a result of a high birth rate and increased legal and illegal immigration.   The

Immigration Act of 1965 admitted 150,000 immigrants annually into the United States from the Western Hemisphere nations. Mexican immigrants made up the largest portion of the Western Hemisphere quota.[74] As the Mexican population grew, new housing, stadiums, office buildings, and the expansion of downtown commercial and civic centers in Southwestern cities divided Chicano barrios and displaced residents.[75] New freeways also divided Chicano neighborhoods, displaced thousands, lowered housing values, and isolated the poor. Those who could afford to relocated to new suburbs, leaving a concentration of poor Mexican Americans and newly arriving Mexican nationals.[76]

Simultaneously, the expansion of industry and housing diminished orchard and cannery jobs in Santa Clara County.[77] Farmers sold their land to developers who built tract housing and strip malls. From 1940 to 1965, agricultural employment fell from 22.6 percent of the total employment in Santa Clara County to just 7 percent. Crop acreage declined by more than 50 percent.[78]

The loss of agricultural work pushed poor migrants into the older central city neighborhoods. During the 1960s, residents of Mexican origin accounted for 25 percent of the city's population increase and 14.5 percent of the city's total. By 1966, Mexican Americans represented nearly 17 percent of San Jose's total population. By 1970, almost 22 percent or approximately 100,000 San Joseans were of Mexican descent.[79]

As poor Mexicans settled in the eastside barrios, they were joined by Chicano students who came to San Jose from throughout the Southwest to attend college at San Jose State University (SJSU), San Jose City College, DeAnza, Ohlone, Santa Clara University, and Stanford.[80] Some benefited from GI programs while others were lured by grants and fellowships. Many came simply because of the advice of friends attending college in San Jose.[81] Some had worked as migrant farmworkers. San Jose State student activist Mauro Chávez came to San Jose from San Diego. The Chicano students at SJSU were in their 20s and 30s, "not kids fresh out of high school," he recalled. Many had served in Vietnam or spent time as farm laborers. Chicanos and Chicanas acknowledged their working class past with pride. Students identified each other by the names of Central Valley or border towns where they had originated, like the "Bakersfield 10" or the "Eagle Pass 12." Chávez said the former farmworkers boasted of having "picked" as a sign of toughness, and the poor Chicanos considered their middle-class Mexican American classmates "illegit."[82]

Despite rising Mexican American university admission percentage rates, Chicanos criticized administrators for moving too slowly to recruit Chicanos. Student activists formed the Student Initiative (SI) in 1965 to help identify, recruit, and lobby for the admission of more Chicano students at SJSU. In the fall of 1966, 12 Chicanos enrolled as part of a program called LEAP (Latent Educational Abilities Program).[83] Finally, Chicanos demanded more Chicano professors and more classes on Mexican history and culture.[84]

Chicanos also became involved in organizing residents in the eastside barrios. The students were influenced by local movements already underway in the barrios. San Jose's sprawling growth had produced pockets of intense poverty as poor migrants settled near downtown in very old housing that received poor city services. A couple of organizations, United People Arriba (UPA) and the Mayfair Action Council, were already active in the eastside barrios. Sophía Mendoza, Juan Brito, Sonny Madrid, and Jorge Alvarez led UPA.[85] Mendoza was born in San Jose but moved to suburban Campbell after she married. She and her husband moved back to the city in the late 1960s and became active in the eastside organizing the poor. Mendoza got into politics at an early age when she accompanied her father while he organized Mexican farmworkers.[86]

UPA included blacks, Mexicans, Puerto Ricans, whites, homeowners, and renters. The group arose when residents complained of poor city services and declining home values after the city annexed eastside neighborhoods but rezoned them for light manufacturing.[87] In unincorporated areas, poor services produced quickly deteriorated streets and houses, which became known as "instant blight." UPA helped deal with bureaucratic entanglements that stood in the way of getting problems solved. San Jose's rapid growth produced a proliferation of government bodies. By the mid 1970s there were 73 local government jurisdictions, 19 special elected boards, 37 school districts, and 25 special districts appointed by the board of supervisors. The multiplication of boards and agencies required that neighborhoods organize to cut through red tape that impeded solutions to neighborhood problems.[88] UPA leafleted, held rallies, and testified at city council meetings. They pressed the city for new sidewalks with gutters, stop signs, and traffic lights in barrio streets. UPA worked to convince residents that they could effect change if they spoke with one voice.

Besides planning issues, Mendoza went door to door speaking with Mexican women about the need to improve local schools. UPA demanded a police review board, improved housing for migrant workers, a medical clinic in the barrio, and an end to discriminatory city hiring. The city officials respected the ability of UPA to mobilize the community in order to influence public policy in the city.[89]

Thus, Chicanos and Chicanas got involved in el movimiento because their neighborhoods in San Jose were fighting the ill effects of urban change. Horizontal growth impoverished the Mexican population. Freeway construction further exacerbated housing overcrowding. Poor city services and bureaucratic red tape produced neighborhood groups that fought to improve eastside conditions. The Chicanos took their studies into the barrios of east San Jose where they joined forces with community groups already active fighting for neighborhood improvements.

CHICANO IDENTITY AND LA FIESTA DE LAS ROSAS

The creation of ethnic identities requires that groups formulate a common understanding of local history. Group cohesion is often strengthened by the existence of an enemy or an opposing ideology. Sometimes the memory of a terrible tragedy forms the basis for a new group unity. Ethnic groups require a creation myth, a history, and important heroes and events to solidify group affiliation.[90]

The Chicano movement was an intensely creative ethnic group formation process. In the 1960s, Chicanos invented a new identity for Mexican Americans that focused on their Native American heritage. They also vilified the Spanish/European history of colonialism and portrayed themselves as culturally victimized by ongoing European American domination. They did so partly to distance themselves from the Mexican American establishment, which they considered too assimilationist and unwilling to push demands that might offend white powerbrokers.

But more than their ethnic identity, the urbanization of the suburbs also influenced their opposition to La Fiesta de las Rosas. Chicanos complained that the event was solely a "business proposition" in which elites used city funds to lure outsiders into downtown while ignoring the needs of local residents. Thus, the creation of the multicentered metropolis, with an extensive freeway system that segregated the poor in barrios near the downtown and created sprawling suburbs that sapped the economic well-being out of the central business district while eliminating agricultural jobs, was more important than ideology in creating the Chicano movement.

The use of the Spanish myth angered Chicanos who rejected any link to European culture and instead identified themselves as non-white or mestizo (mixed blood). They constructed a cultural identity based on Chicano resistance to Spanish and Anglo imperialism and racism. They rejected any suggestion that Mexicans and Spaniards had a common historical experience, which was a central message of the fiesta's pan-Latino perspective.

The concept of "Aztlán" was at the heart of the Chicano ideology. "Aztlán" referred to the Southwest in general, but particularly to the land lost by Mexico in 1848. Aztec mythology said the Aztecs had migrated to central Mexico from "the north," which Chicanos took to mean the Southwestern United States.[91] Reconceptualizing the Southwest as Aztlán allowed Chicanos to claim the region as their homeland and refute the idea that Mexican Americans were newcomers to the United States. The Aztlán concept also underscored the cultural ties linking Chicanos and Mexican immigrants. Finally, Aztlán identified Chicanos as non-whites with an indigenous rather than European cultural heritage.[92]

Their indigenous identity allowed Chicanos to claim that they were the victims of Spanish and then American colonialism. Thus, Chicanos were similar to yet different from other Latino groups. They, unlike other South and Central Americans, had their land appropriated by Anglos after the Mexican War in 1848. In the 1960s, with increased numbers of Cubans, Colombians, Nicaraguans, and other Latin Americans in the United States, Chicanos used Aztlán to clearly delineate the special history of Mexicans and Chicanos in the Southwest.[93]

While declaring themselves mestizos, and thus the result of the Spanish conquest of native Americans, they viewed the conquest as violent and genocidal, and downplayed or ignored their European heritage. They concluded that working-class, darker skinned Mexicans were predominantly Indian by blood and culture. This perspective reversed that of Mexicans who ignored their Indian heritage and embraced a Spanish identity in the attempt, often fruitless, to avoid anti-Mexican discrimination. Chicanos hated the Spanish myth because it countered all their efforts to create pride in their non-white identity. It placed them on the side of the Spanish and Anglos as the erasers of Indian and Mexican history. Thus, they rejected the fiesta which "glorified, in Anglo tradition, the Spanish conquest of the native Indian and his civilization" and "the vicious exploitation of the mestizo [Mexican] by the Spaniard." The fiesta celebrated Spanish missionaries and conquistadores thus suggesting the "inferiority of the Chicano that presently is believed by a large segment of society."[94]

Chicanos understood that suburbanization had left San Jose's downtown in decline. The festival, they argued, was designed to "give life to dying downtown business at the expense of the taxpayer."[95] The event was planned largely by Anglos who wanted to appropriate Mexican American history to help revitalize the downtown. The city spent public funds for an event that produced a stereotypical image of Chicano history, thus giving official sanction to those stereotypes.

Chicanos opposed the Spanish myth for obscuring the Mexican community's historic struggle against the racism of white Europeans. They also saw the myth as encouraging Mexicans to assimilate into the Anglo mainstream rather than retain their mestizo identity. One activist noted, "this is our country," perhaps referring to the mythical land of Aztlán, "it was built by Mexicans and Mestizos. It's about time people got the facts straight."[96] Another Chicano noted, "the missions were built mainly by Indian labor. It really irks me to see all the fanfare about the Spanish, when the real work of the Indians goes unrecognized."[97]

The Fiesta de las Rosas parade confrontation culminated a series of actions by young Chicanos who opposed the celebration. Several weeks before opening day, the Mexican American Student Confederation (MASC) called for San Jose's Mexican American community to boycott the fiesta. On the fiesta's opening day, about one hundred Chicanos marched and chanted slogans during the coronation of the fiesta's Anglo queen.[98]

Chicanos realized they had to work to overcome the Spanish myth and the association of Mexican and Spanish history. They struggled to get Mexican Americans to support an identity that resisted Anglo domination. To instill ethnic pride, Chicanos stressed the necessity of writing their own history to counter the Spanish myth: "We are no longer going to turn the other cheek to insults . . . we know and understand ourselves, our history better than anyone else."[99]   Only accurate history could refute the falsehoods that prevailed in the fiestas and festivals that flourished after World War II in cities throughout the region.

The major source of conflict during the San Jose festival concerned the representation of Chicano history. The fiesta committee invested public funds for the production of a commemorative medallion featuring the images of a Spanish missionary and a conquistador. Chicano activists sued the city to stop the use of public money for the medallion, which they argued celebrated their "conquest and enslavement by the Spanish conquistadors" and represented official city approval of Spanish exploitation of Native Americans and Mexicans. The activists hired historians Octavio Romano and Feliciano Rivera as expert witnesses to help establish the accuracy of their reading of the historical record.[100]

Chicanos denounced the medallion because it featured two institutions they most resented: the military (symbolized by the conquistador) and the church (symbolized by the missionary). Chicanos held the military and the church responsible for the oppression of Mexican Americans in the past and present. They staunchly opposed the appearance of military personnel and church officials in the parade.[101] They blasted the Catholic church for taking money from the community without providing adequate social services in return.[102] They blamed the Spanish missionaries for forcing the Native Americans to assimilate to Spanish culture, a process analogous to current demands that Mexicans adopt Anglo traditions.[103] They demanded that the archdiocese of San Francisco fund social action programs in the Mexican American community.[104] Similarly, they criticized the U.S. military for using minorities on the front lines out of proportion to their numbers in the general population of the United States.[105]

PAN-LATINO VS. CHICANO PERSPECTIVES ON LA FIESTA

Despite the city's insistence that the fiesta celebrated San Jose's ethnic diversity, Chicanos said it misrepresented their history. As sociologist Iwona Irwin-Zarecka argues, conflicts over the articulation of history arise for many different reasons. Differences about history often lead to hostilities when a group feels that past crimes have gone unacknowledged or even celebrated. Native Americans criticized the events surrounding the 500th anniversary of Columbus' discovery because no adequate acknowledgement was given to the millions of indigenous people who perished as a result of the European conquest. The celebration benefited those who had already profited from the conquest and victimized once again the indigenous population. But the opposition to the quincentenary events contributed to the formation of a collective Native American identity. As Irwin-Zarecka notes, "caring for the past is always coupled with having someone challenge your vision of it."[106]

Chicanos opposed La Fiesta de las Rosas because they felt that the celebration of Spanish culture represented support for the oppression of Native Americans and Chicanos, the victims of the European conquest and subsequent colonization. As one Chicano stated, "early California was built by the slave labor of the Mexican and the Indian."[107] Rather than acknowledge their victimization, the fiesta praised the victimizers, the Spanish. Zarecka explains that "when killings, expulsion, oppression go unacknowledged, when these bring rewards rather than punishments, when those responsible are allowed the comforts of forgetting, the wounds remain open."[108]

The fiesta exemplified a pan-Latino perspective that collapsed Mexican and Spanish histories and cultures. This merging of two traditions argued for the essential common history and culture of the oppressor and the oppressed. The fiesta placed Mexicans, or mestizos, side-by-side the Spanish. The fiesta celebrated the Spanish conquest and failed to acknowledge those victimized by Spanish colonialism. By including Mexican history and culture, the event served to represent Mexicans as partners in the conquest rather than the victims of that conquest.

The fiesta's multiculturalism suggested that Spanish, Mexican, and Anglo histories were not in conflict. The fiesta avoided important distinctions between victimizers and victims in order to unify San Jose residents. The Chicanos viewed Spaniards and Anglo Americans as imperialists who victimized Mexicans. By celebrating the Latino community's diversity and essential unity, fiesta planners placed Chicanos on the side of the victimizers.

Yet in criticizing the Spanish myth and the pan-Latino identity, Chicanos ignored the role of Mexicans in founding the original settlements that grew into Southwestern cities. Because they understood the Spanish incursion into the Southwest as entirely negative, Chicanos failed to acknowledge early Mexican participation in the founding of the cities. Mexican Americans, on the other hand, saw Spanish colonization as part of their heritage and, particularly, an important part of San Jose's history that should be celebrated.

CONCLUSION

The rhetoric of the culture wars is geared toward sound bites. The opposing sides simplify, exaggerate, and distort the arguments of their adversaries. Nowhere is this problem more evident than in the debate over the representation of American history. One of the most intense recent controversies concerned the exhibit at the Smithsonian Museum on the dropping of the atom bomb on Japan ending World War II. Veterans groups demanded that the curators revise the presentation to emphasize the atrocities perpetrated by the Japanese military. Even after museum officials revised the exhibit and it received approval from veteran consultants, demagogic right-wing politicians denounced the museum staff as "anti-American."[109]

The conflict covered here about the Fiesta de las Rosas demonstrates the connection between urban change and the search for a useable history. As San Jose grew, its leaders wanted a high density, vibrant downtown where people could meet and where the city could project its urban image. Professional Mexican Americans who desired to see the city prosper also supported the fiesta's revival. They were proud of their city and believed that their own success stemmed from the city's growth. They believed that the city could benefit by utilizing its Hispanic past to sharpen its urban image. They also wanted to increase awareness among all San Jose residents about the Latino contributions to the city. They attempted to use the Spanish myth to counter the general population's failure to recognize Mexican participation in the growth of California and the West.

After the fiesta, Luis Juárez defended the Spanish against criticism. While Anglos largely exterminated the Native Americans, he noted, the Spanish "were influenced by the padres ever present . . . who believed that the most important mandate from the Spanish throne was to save the souls of the heathen inhabitants of the new world." Therefore, even though "no one can say that the tactics used by the conquering Spaniards . . . should be condoned, unlike the conquerors of the northern lands, they intermarried with the Indian, thus giving way to a 'mestizo' population, the Mexican."[110] By praising both Mexican and Spanish history and culture he exemplified a "pan-Latino" identity.

Anglo and Mexican Americans attempted to use the Spanish myth to lure visitors to the downtown but Chicanos opposed that strategy. They understood, as sociologist Sharon Zukin has argued, that cultural symbols generated "real economic power."[111] Redevelopment foretold displacement of poor residents by hotels, shopping areas, and upscale restaurants. History was not an amenity but an essential element in modernizing downtown San Jose for use by more outsiders.

The fiesta not only failed to unite San Jose residents but divided them further. Chicanos were not the only ones to criticize the city's focus on the Spanish and Anglo settlement of the West. Increasingly, non-Hispanic whites rejected historical references that they considered too "foreign" and that they felt indicated a lack of assimilation. After the fiesta demonstration, one Anglo resident insisted:

It's time to realize we are all Americans and should act like Americans instead of acting like the country you came from was so good. Why didn't the people that start trouble here stay in their native country instead of causing upsets here? We should change the Fiesta de las Rosas name to a good American name as "The Gala Parade of Fun and Roses" or any name you pick or the Public wants for our American name. . . . The streets and Avenues should have good American names, too.[112]

The conflict did not sidetrack the search for a common historical identity, and into the 1970s, planners insisted that "all opportunity should be used to emphasize the community's cultural background."[113] However, deciding what was the city's "cultural background" remains a question today.

The conflict over history in San Jose shows that groups are concerned about the representation of their past, not just because they seek to raise group self-esteem, as some critics of multiculturalism contend. Rather, history is part of the struggle for power within cities and suburbs undergoing rapid change. Metropolitan growth inevitably produces the search for a place's "roots," but the rise of multicultural communities challenges any attempt to produce an official local history. Even within groups, different historical perspectives exist. Some Mexican Americans embraced a "Hispanic" or pan-Latino perspective while Chicanos wanted to differentiate clearly Mexicans and Spaniards.[114]

The view of the Chicanos ultimately prevailed largely because many within the Mexican American community admired the political commitment and forceful activism of the young people. By the late 1960s, many resented the government's continued blindness to the needs of the community. The weakening of national borders makes history more contentious then ever before. Nations react to new immigrants by shoring up their national identities. They create "official" histories that strengthen an imagined core identity while excluding newcomers.[115] But not just nations do this. In the 1960s, suburbs grew into cities and cities suburbanized, and the collapse of clear urban-suburban distinctions produced conflicts over history. The next chapter looks at Concord, a former suburb that evolved into an "edge city," which produced clashes over the use of modern art and local history to promote economic growth.

NOTES

1. *San Jose Mercury-News*, June 1, 1969.
2. Reports of the clash appeared in the *Mercury-News* and in the *San Francisco Chronicle*, June 2, 1969. On the injured demonstrators, see *Mercury-News*, June 3, 1969; June 4, 1969.
3. *Mercury-News*, June 3, 1969.
4. *Chronicle*, June 2, 1969.
5. *Mercury-News*, June 3, 1969.
6. *San Jose Maverick*, July 1969.
7. Oral history transcript, Frances Palacios, Chicano Studies Center, San Jose State University, 1989; Arturo Villarreal, "Black Berets for Justice" (master's thesis, San Jose State University, 1991), 97; Louis Hernandez Rocha, "Chicano/Mexicano History in San Jose, California and the Press, 1965-1975" (unpublished paper, San Jose State University, 1991), 46–47.
8. *San Jose News*, May 16, 1969.
9. See Timothy P. Fong, *The First Suburban Chinatown: The Remaking of Monterey Park, California* (Philadelphia, 1994); William H. Frey and William P. O'Hare, "Vivan Los Suburbios," *American Demographics* 15 (April 1993): 30–37.
10. See Arthur M. Schlesinger, Jr., *The Disuniting of America: Reflections on a Multicultural Society* (New York, 1992).
11. See Todd Gitlin, *The Twilight of Common Dreams: Why America Is Wracked by the Culture Wars* (New York, 1995), 7–36.
12. See David Lowenthal, *The Past Is a Foreign Country* (New York, 1985); Eric Hobsbawm and Terence Ranger, eds., *The Invention of Tradition* (New York, 1983); John E. Bodnar, *Remaking America: Public Memory, Commemoration, and Patriotism in the Twentieth Century* (Princeton, 1992).
13. See August Meier and Elliott Rudwick, *Black History and the Historical Profession, 1915-80* (Urbana, 1986).
14. See James B. Gardner and George Rollie Adams, eds., *Ordinary People and Everyday Life: Perspectives on the New Social History* (Nashville, 1983).
15. See Schlesinger, *Disuniting of America*, 80.
16. See for example, Dolores Hayden, *The Power of Place: Urban Landscapes as Public History* (Cambridge, 1995).
17. Frederic Hall, *The History of San Jose and Surroundings: With Biographical Sketches of Early Settlers* (San Francisco, 1871); Oscar Osburn Winther, *The Story of San Jose, 1777-1869, California's First Pueblo* (San Francisco, 1935); Clyde Arbuckle, *Clyde Arbuckle's History of San Jose* (San Jose, 1986).
18. Patricia Zavella, *Women's Work and Chicano Families: Cannery Workers of the Santa Clara Valley* (Ithaca, 1987), 51–52. See also Robert James Claus, "The Fruit and Vegetable Canning Industry in the Santa Clara Valley," (master's thesis, San Jose State College, 1966).
19. Charles S. McCaleb, *Tracks, Tires and Wires: Public Transportation in California's Santa Clara Valley* (Glendale, 1981), 2–4.
20. San Jose City Planning Commission, *Master Plan for San Jose* (San Jose, 1964);

Charles M. Coleman, *P.G.&E of California: The Centennial Story of Pacific Gas and Electric Company 1852-1952* (New York, 1952), 172.

21.   *Commercial History of San Jose, California* (San Francisco, 1892), 33.

22.   Stanford Environmental Law Society, *San Jose: Sprawling City-A Report on Land Use Politics and Practices in San Jose, California* (Palo Alto, 1971),

23.   Charles Wollenberg, *Golden Gate Metropolis: Perspectives on Bay Area History* (Berkeley, 1985), 257–261.

24.   County Santa Clara Planning Department, *A Study of the Economy of Santa Clara County, California part 1* (San Jose, 1967), 9–10; AnnaLee Saxenian, "The Urban Contradictions of Silicon Valley: Regional Growth and the Restructuring of the Semiconductor Industry," in Larry Sawers and William K. Tabb, eds., *Sunbelt/Snowbelt: Urban Development and Regional Restructuring* (New York, 1983), 163–197; Donald N. Rothblatt, "The San Jose Metropolitan Area: A Region in Transition," (working paper 90–22, Institute of Governmental Studies, University of California-Berkeley, 1990), 2–3.

25.   *San Jose: Sprawling City*, 6; Philip J. Trounstine, *Movers and Shakers: The Study of Community Power* (New York, 1982).

26.   Arbuckle, *History of San Jose*, 62–63.

27.   Peter A. Morrison, *San Jose and St. Louis in the 1960s: A Case Study of Changing Urban Populations* (Santa Monica, 1973), 11.

28.   *Master Plan for San Jose*, 74.

29.   San Jose Planning Department, *Urban Design Plan: Preliminary Report, September 1976* (San Jose, 1976), 1–2; John M. Findlay, *Magic Lands: Western Cityscapes and American Culture After 1940* (Berkeley, 1992), 38–39.

30.   *San Jose: Sprawling City*, 6.

31.   For criticism of San Jose's growth, see Richard Reinhardt, "Joe Ridder's San Jose," *San Francisco Magazine* (November 1965); Karl Belser, "The Making of Slurban America," *Cry California* 15 (Fall 1970): 1–21; and *San Jose: Sprawling City*, 5–15.

32.   *Master Plan for San Jose*, 71.

33.   Ibid., 29, 58.

34.   San Jose Department of Planning, *San Jose Core Area Study: An Analysis and Evaluation of Past Studies, Existing Conditions, and Constraints* (San Jose, 1970), 78.

35.   *Mercury-News*, October 17, 1966.

36.   Mary Jeanne Sauerwein, President, Fiesta Board of Directors, *Official Program: La Fiesta de las Rosas* (San Jose, 1969), 23.

37.   Ibid., 15.

38.   On the Spanish myth, see Carey McWilliams, *North from Mexico: The Spanish-Speaking People of the United States* (New York, 1948), 35–47; David Weber, *The Spanish Frontier in Northern America* (New Haven, 1992), 335–360; Leonard Pitt, *The Decline of the Californios: A Social History of the Spanish-Speaking Californians, 1846-1890* (Berkeley, 1966), 277–296.

39.   John R. Chávez, *The Lost Land: The Chicano Image of the Southwest* (Albuquerque, 1984), 89–102.

40.   *Mercury-News*, September 18, 1966.

41.   See Mario T. García, *Mexican Americans: Leadership, Ideology, and Identity, 1930-1960* (New Haven, 1989); George J. Sánchez, *Becoming Mexican American: Ethnicity, Culture, and Identity in Chicano Los Angeles, 1900-1945* (New York, 1993); David G. Gutiérrez, *Walls and Mirrors: Mexican Americans, Mexican Immigrants, and the Politics of Ethnicity* (Berkeley, 1996).

42.   On LULAC, see Benjamin Márquez, *LULAC: The Evolution of a Mexican American Political Organization* (Austin, 1993). On the G.I. Forum, see Carl Allsop, *The American G.I. Forum: Origins and Evolution* (Austin, 1982).

43.   United States Bureau of the Census, *Nineteenth Census, 1970, Occupation of Employed Persons by Class of Worker, Race, and Sex, 1970* (Washington D.C., 1972), 1696,

1698.

44.   Diane Adele Trombetta Reynolds, "Economic Integration and Cultural Assimilation: Mexican Americans in San Jose" (Ph.D. dissertation, Stanford University, 1974), 26–27.

45.   Luis G. Juárez, interview by author, June 13, 1990.

46.   *Mercury-News*, August 8, 1965.

47.   *Mercury-News*, September 24, 1967.

48.   Laurie Kay Sommers, "Inventing Latinismo: The Creation of 'Hispanic' Panethnicity in the United States," *Journal of American Folklore* 104 (1991): 32–53.

49.   David G. Gutiérrez notes that "only a tiny fraction" of Spanish speakers in the Southwest after 1848 were pure blooded Spaniards, in Gutiérrez, *Walls and Mirrors*, 33. Matt S. Meier and Feliciano Ribera claim that most of the upper-class land grant holders in California were "peninsular Spaniards or criollos, a few were mestizos or mulattoes," in Meier and Ribera, *Mexican Americans American Mexicans* rev. ed. (New York, 1993), 44–45. On Hispanos, see Alvar W. Carlson, *The Spanish-American Homeland: Four Centuries of New Mexico's Rio Arriba* (Baltimore, 1990).

50.   See Sánchez, *Becoming Mexican American*, 108; and Jose Amaro Hernandez, *Mutual Aid for Survival: The Case of the Mexican American* (Malabar, 1983), 34.

51.   See *El Espectador*, December 12, 1947. In the 1940s, the paper's masthead featured the image of a Spanish mission.

52.   Quoted in Gutiérrez, *Walls and Mirrors*, 76.

53.   Quoted in Sánchez, *Becoming Mexican American*, 247.

54.   *Mercury-News*, August 8, 1965.

55.   Joseph A. Rodriguez, "Becoming Latino: Mexican Americans, Chicanos, and the Spanish Myth in the Urban Southwest," *Western Historical Quarterly* 29 (Summer 1998): 165–185

56.   *Mercury-News*, September 24, 1967. Olvera Street, the old central plaza of the Spanish/Mexican pueblo, is now a tourist site where vendors sell handicrafts.

57.   *Mercury-News*, February 16, 1967.

58.   Ibid.

59.   *Official Program: La Fiesta de las Rosas*, 44.

60.   On the Chicano movement see Carlos Muñoz, *Youth, Identity, Power: The Chicano Movement* (London, 1989); Armando Navarro, *The Cristal Experiment: A Chicano Struggle for Community Control* (Madison, 1998); Carlos Muñoz and Mario Barrera, "La Raza Unida Party and the Chicano Student Movement," *Social Science Journal* 19 (1982): 101–119; Juan Gómez-Quiñones, *Chicano Politics: Reality and Promise 1940-1990* (Albuquerque, 1990); Juan Gómez-Quiñones, *Students Por La Raza: The Chicano Student Movement in Southern California, 1967-1977* (Santa Barbara, 1978); Paul Rosen, *Political Ideology and the Chicano Movement: A Study of the Political Ideology of the Activists in the Chicano Movement* (San Francisco, 1975); Ramón A. Gutiérrez, "Community, Patriarchy and Individualism: The Politics of Chicano History and the Dream of Equality," *American Quarterly* 45, no. 1 (March 1993): 44–72; Edward J. Escobar, "The Dialectics of Repression: The Los Angeles Police Department and the Chicano Movement, 1968-1971," *Journal of American History* 79, no. 4 (March 1993): 1483-1514.

61.   Navarro, *The Cristal Experiment*, 382.

62.   Though many were probably mestizos, New Mexican tenant farmers called themselves "Hispanos" and traced their ancestry to the early Spanish settlers.

63.   On Tijerina see Rudy Val Busto, "Like a Mighty Rushing Wind: The Religious Impulse in the Life and Writing of Reies López Tijerina," (Ph.D. dissertation, University of California-Berkeley, 1991); Patricia Bell Blawis, *Tijerina and the Land Grants: Mexican Americans and the Struggle for their Heritage* (New York, 1971); Richard Cummings, *Grito! Tijerina and the New Mexico Land Grant War of 1967* (New York, 1971); Peter Nabokov, *Tijerina and the Courthouse Raid* (Albuquerque, 1971).

64.   On Chávez, see Richard Griswold del Castillo and Richard A. García, *César Chávez: A Triumph of Spirit* (Norman, 1995).

65.   Ignacio M. García, *Chicanismo: The Forging of a Militant Ethos Among Mexican Americans* (Tucson, 1997). On Corky Gonzales, see Christine Marin, *A Spokesman of the Mexican American Movement: Rodolfo "Corky" Gonzales and the Fight for Chicano Liberation, 1966-1972* (San Francisco, 1977).

66.   See Ignacio M. García, *United We Win: The Rise and Fall of La Raza Unida Party* (Tucson, 1989).

67.   See David G. Gutiérrez, "Sin Fronteras?: Chicanos, Mexican Americans, and the Emergence of the Contemporary Mexican Immigration Debate, 1968-1978," *Journal of American Ethnic History* 10, no. 4 (Summer 1991): 5–37.

68.   Escobar, "Dialectics of Repression," 1492.

69.   Ibid., 1501.

70.   Russ Sommers, "An Affirmation of Political Socialization and Institutional Change Through Citizen Participation in the San Jose California Model Cities Program: A Case Study" (master's thesis, San Jose State University, 1974), 125. See also Nancy L. Geilhufe, *Chicanos and the Police: A Study of the Politics of Ethnicity in San Jose, California* (Washington D.C., 1979), 6.

71.   On Chicano murals, see Eva Sperling Cockcroft and Holly Barnet-Sánchez, eds., *Signs from the Heart: California Chicano Murals* (Albuquerque, 1990).

72.   See for example Ricardo Romo, *East Los Angeles: History of a Barrio* (Austin, 1983), 79–82.

73.   Sánchez, *Becoming Mexican American*, 76–77.

74.   David Reimers, *Still the Golden Door: The Third World Comes to America* (New York, 1985), 131.

75.   Joan Moore and Raquel Pinderhughes, eds., *In the Barrios: Latinos and the Underclass Debate* (New York, 1993).

76.   See Rodolfo F. Acuña, *A Community Under Siege: A Chronicle of Chicanos East of the Los Angeles River, 1945-1975* (Los Angeles, 1984).

77.   Barbara Joan Oskoni, "The Police, the Public, and the Mass Media" (master's thesis, San Jose State University, 1980), 284; Zavella, *Women's Work and Chicano Families*, 52–53.

78.   Paul Conrad Huszar, "On the Rationale of Urban Growth: A Behavioral Study of San Jose, California" (Ph.D dissertation, University of California-Berkeley, 1972), 51–57, 127.

79.   United States Bureau of the Census, *Nineteenth Census 1970, Table 153, California* (Washington D.C., 1972), 1333.

80.   Juan Oliverez, "Chicano Student Activism at San Jose State College, 1967-1972: An Analysis of Ideology, Leadership, and Change" (Ph.D. dissertation, University of California-Berkeley), 10–11.

81.   Yaya De Luna Martinez, "A Five Year Study of Chicano Educational Opportunity Students at a California State University" (Ph.D. dissertation, University of Southern California, 1976), 34; Francis Palacios, Humberto Garza oral history transcripts, Chicano Studies Center, San Jose State University.

82.   Mauro Chávez, interview by the author, January 7, 1992.

83.   Martinez, "A Five Year Study of Chicano Educational Opportunity Students," 37, 40.

84.   See *Mercury-News*, September 17, 1969.

85.   Sophía Mendoza, interview by the author, January 10, 1991.

86.   Ibid.

87.   Russ Sommers, "An Affirmation of Political Socialization," 82.

88.   Ibid., 53.

89.   Sophía Mendoza interview.

90.   The literature on ethnic group identity formation is voluminous. But I have found most helpful Iwona Irwin-Zarecka, *Frames of Remembrance: The Dynamics of Collective Memory* (New Brunswick, 1994; Mary C. Waters, *Ethnic Options: Choosing Identities in America* (Berkeley, 1990); Karen Leonard, *Making Ethnic Choices: California's Punjabi Mexican Americans* (Philadelphia, 1992).

91.   This story has some basis in fact. Marc Simmons notes that Southwestern Indians believed Montezuma was born in New Mexico. See Simmons, *Witchcraft in the Southwest* (Lincoln, 1974), 127.

92.   See John R. Chávez, *The Lost Land*, 129-130; Navarro, *The Cristal Experiment*, xi; Muñoz, *Youth, Identity, Power*, 77; Ignacio M. García, *United We Win*, 95.

93.   Small numbers of immigrants from various regions may unite behind broad national identities. Larger populations of immigrants, however, may separate into regional factions, which replace the broad national identity. See Jean Bacon, *Life Lines: Community, Family, and Assimilation Among Asian Indian Immigrants* (New York, 1996), 26.

94.   "La Fiesta de las Rosas: An Analysis," *La Palabra* 1, no. 1 (November 1, 1969): 10–11.

95.   Ibid.

96.   *Mercury-News*, April 19, 1969.

97.   *Oakland Tribune*, October 19, 1969.

98.   Luis G. Juárez, interview by the author.

99.   "La Fiesta de las Rosas: An Analysis," 10–11.

100.   City of San Jose Memorandum #221837, San Jose City Council, August 25, 1969. La Confederación de la Raza dropped the suit following the fiesta as planners agreed to format changes.

101.   *Mercury-News*, April 19, 1969.

102.   Chicanos in Santa Clara asserted that the Catholic church owed the community $350,000. They claimed that while the archdiocese held $500 million worth of real estate in the county, it gave only $50,000 per year for barrio services. See *Catholic Voice*, May 28, 1969.

103.   Catholic authorities caved from grower pressure and denounced priests who helped organize farmworkers in the Central Valley. See Moíses Sandoval, "The Church and El Movimiento," in Sandoval, ed., *Fronteras: A History of the Latin American Church in the USA Since 1513* (San Antonio, 1983), 377–410.

104.   *Mercury-News*, May 16, 1969.

105.   Following the 1969 fiesta, Chicanos demanded the exclusion of any military personnel from future celebrations, *Mercury-News*, October 1, 1970.

106.   Irwin-Zarecka, *Frames of Remembrance*, 76.

107.   *San Jose Sun*, no date on clipping.

108.   Irwin-Zarecka, *Frames of Remembrance*, 77.

109.   See the summary of the controversy in Mike Wallace, *Mickey Mouse History and Other Essays on American Memory* (Philadelphia, 1996). See also the articles in a roundtable on the Enola Gay controversy in *Journal of American History* 82, no. 3 (December 1995): 1029–1135.

110.   *Mercury-News*, June 6, 1971.

111.   Sharon Zukin, "Space and Symbols in an Age of Decline," in Anthony D. King, ed., *Re-presenting the City: Ethnicity, Capital and Culture in the 21st Century Metropolis* (New York, 1996), 44. Zukin notes that "no matter how restricted the definition of art that is implied, or how few artists are included or how little the benefits extend to other social groups outside certain segments of the middle class, the visibility and viability of a city's symbolic economy plays an important role in the creation of place." (45)

112.   Letter from M. Hoffman to San Jose City Council, August 18, 1969, Fiesta de las Rosas, file 8323, San Jose City Clerk's Office.

113.   *San Jose Core Area Study*, 165.

114.   Alex M. Saragoza, "Recent Chicano Historiography: An Interpretive Essay," *Aztlán* 19, no. 1 (Spring 1988-1990): 1–77.

115.   See for example Blair A. Ruble, *Money Sings: The Changing Politics of Urban Space in Post-Soviet Yaroslavl* (New York, 1995).

4

PUBLIC ART IN CONCORD

On November 5, 1985, a gay black man was found hung near the Concord BART station. The police ruled his death a suicide but the deceased's family demanded an investigation. That same night two white men wearing Ku Klux Klan robes and carrying Klan membership cards stabbed two black men in Concord. Following these incidents, the California Civil Rights Commission investigated racism in eastern Contra Costa County. Numerous minority residents testified to having experienced racial slurs, beatings, vandalism, and employment and housing discrimination in Concord. The commission concluded that 20 to 30 Concord residents were members of white supremacy groups. After the hearings, Concord Mayor Ron Mullin admitted that Concord had "ignored the minority part of our community until now. It's hard to be a minority here."[1]

Racial hostility in Concord was a growing problem in the 1980s. Though often stereotyped as bedroom communities, many American suburbs like Concord have grown to become self-sufficient cities. They boast thriving downtown districts where new buildings house large corporations employing urban and suburban workers who commute to their suburban jobs each day. These downtowns also include new theaters, performing arts centers, and museums. The new suburban offices attract diverse workers, some of whom settle permanently in the community.[2]

While many have noted the urbanization of the suburbs, there is little analysis of the conflicts that this transformation generates.[3] The economic success of suburban cities often obscures the accompanying social friction. Like cities, suburbs now have their own racial problems. Besides racial problems, urbanizing suburbs become sites for cultural conflicts also. Urbanization challenges the suburb's original identity as a bedroom community. In Concord, after World War II, real estate developers publicized the community as a good place for young families. Developers established homeowner associations that encouraged grassroots participation in local government. But by the 1970s, urbanization required that Concord hire professionals to grapple with the community's rapid growth. While some residents favored the transition to an "edge city," others feared that urbanization undermined Concord's traditional support for local families.

In the 1980s, the city leaders funded two public art projects to demonstrate that Concord had arrived as a metropolis. They also hoped to use art to draw more upscale businesses, affluent shoppers, and other outsiders to energize downtown Concord. BART brought professionals into the city to new office buildings in downtown. But many left Concord immediately after work. Thus, modern public art both re-flected Concord's recent urbanization and promoted further growth by giving the downtown an upscale image.[4] As the downtown gentrified, city leaders hoped professionals would spend their leisure time and money in the suburb rather than in San Francisco or Oakland.

In the late 1980s, Concord officials commissioned a large modern sculpture to represent the city's past and present. Dubbed the "Spirit Poles," the piece enraged local residents not only because it offended their aesthetic sensibilities but because, they felt, it did not accurately represent the community's history. They also expressed their displeasure with plans to rehabilitate the town's central plaza. They wrote numerous letters to local newspapers opposing both the sculpture and the plans for the redesigned plaza, and they ousted three city council members who supported the projects.[5]

In today's culture wars, conservatives vilify avant garde art they consider obscene. In 1989, under pressure by conservative members, Congress nearly jettisoned funding for the National Endowment for the Arts (NEA). Conservatives launched an attack on the agency for funding such artists as Robert Mapplethorpe, known for his graphic photographs of gay male sexuality, and Andres Serrano, famous for his photograph of a crucifix submerged in urine entitled "Piss Christ."[6] Christians criticized the NEA for funding such artists whose work they found offensive.[7] The positive response of art critics to the work of Mapplethorpe and Serrano enraged conservatives who saw this celebration of prurient art as indicative of the nation's growing inability to distinguish moral and immoral forms of expression. In contrast, progressives claimed that these efforts to stop funding for contemporary art amounted to censorship, suppression of freedom of speech, and undue religious influence over the spending of public money.[8]

While these national conflicts over art exhibits drew headlines, local communities became embroiled in heated struggles over public art. Public art is controversial because it raises the question of who has the authority to decide public taste. Public art also implies that local residents approve of it. Public artists produce large sculptures to force the viewer to ponder complex ideas. Richard Serra placed a giant piece of iron called "Tilted Arc" in the middle of Manhattan Federal Plaza in New York to raise questions about who had control over urban space.[9] Art historian Erika Doss has noted that "controversies over public art style really unmask deeper concerns Americans have regarding their voice in the public sphere."[10] In short, who decides what goes where? Who decides what is art? Does the public have a voice equal to art experts and the artists themselves?

Many Americans respond negatively to public artists who claim to speak for "the people," especially when these artists produce works that mock religious, family, and patriotic values. As art has become more abstract and is often aimed only at inciting the viewer, art experts and artists have lost their legitimacy as social critics. In the past, much of art criticized social inequalities. But since city leaders now use art as part of their strategy for urban redevelopment, it faces criticism for being geared toward outsiders and therefore out of touch with common people.[11]

In Concord, controversies over public art stemmed from a growing sense that urbanization placed the interests of outsiders over locals. Gleaming new high-rises built by corporations like Bank of America and Wells Fargo Bank proliferated downtown in the 1980s. Increased development brought more traffic and higher rents. As real estate values increased, upscale establishments replaced locally owned outlets. The sense of Concord as a residential suburb diminished, and the cityscape no longer seemed to reflect the history or character of the town's early residents.

These changes led some older residents to see public art as another area in which they had lost control of their community. The suburb's original builders had emphasized community participation and support for family traditions. Developers encouraged residents to become involved in the suburb's governance. The urbanization of the suburb amounted to their displacement. Among the residents opposed to the projects were old-timers who sought to regain some control over city development. Urbanization, by requiring the growth of a group of municipal professionals who worked with developers, seemed to be taking the power over local growth out of the hands of residents and giving it to experts interested in attracting outsiders.

HISTORICAL BACKGROUND

Concord is located in Contra Costa County east of the East Bay hills. Contra Costa County is divided into two parts, the bayside portion from

Richmond to Pittsburg and the central portion of Concord, Walnut Creek, Danville, Alamo, San Ramon, Pleasanton, Orinda, and Lafayette. These central county towns are located along the old Mission Road that connected Martinez north to the gold fields and south to San Jose and Monterey. The East Bay hills limited interaction between the central county and the East Bay, Oakland, and San Francisco until the 1930s.[12]

In the nineteenth century, the central county was mostly an agricultural area. Farmers sent crops north to Martinez and south to San Jose. Martinez was one of the earliest towns in the Bay Area. Located at the Carquinez Straits, Martinez was an overnight stop where boats ferried passengers across the Bay's waters.[13] Farmers in the area exported grain until the late 1800s, then planted orchards and vegetable fields, which they augmented with vineyards. Don Salvio Pacheco laid out a town in what became central county in the 1840s called Todos Santos, which later became Pacheco. By the mid 1800s, Pacheco was a grain shipping center with flour mills and warehouses until it was destroyed by flooding in 1862. After the floods, Pacheco residents moved to a new town platted in 1869 by Pacheco businessmen, which became Concord.[14]

The East Bay hills limited development of the interior even after the coming of interurban railroad in 1910. But the population grew more rapidly along the bayshore where county residents worked at the refineries in Martinez. These included Standard Oil (1901), Avon (1911), and Shell Oil (1913). A Columbia Steel plant was built in nearby Pittsburg in 1910.[15]

Central Contra Costa County also lured city people seeking a rural retreat from the big metropolis. San Francisco businessmen began building large estates in central county in the 1920s. They were attracted by good weather, the beauty of the area, and the serenity of the rural atmosphere. Along with mansions, the wealthy city folks built country clubs both to overcome the area's isolation and for status purposes. Mt. Diablo Estate included a country club, along with a community farm, dairy and poultry yard, and playground and a little zoo.[16] But the East Bay hills meant few commuted to San Francisco or Oakland. Because of isolation, the towns developed their own local institutions, including stores and newspapers. The construction of the Caldecott Tunnel and the Bay Bridge in the 1930s brought more development. A new modern highway linked central Contra Costa County to Berkeley, Oakland, and San Francisco, cutting the commute to the East Bay and San Francisco in half.

THE MARAVILLA DEVELOPMENT:
CREATING A SUBURBAN COMMUNITY

After World War II, central Contra Costa County became a center of rapid suburban growth. Returning veterans and others who had migrated to California during the war purchased economically priced single-family houses in the area. The Federal Housing Administration (FHA) and the Veterans Administration (VA) guaranteed low-interest loans, which made it possible for returning GIs to purchase newly constructed homes. The military's continued post-war presence in the area also spurred migration to the suburbs. Concord's growth owed directly to its proximity to Buchanan Field, Mare Island, and Port Chicago. Buchanan Field, where Aircobra pilots received advanced training, was established in 1942. In 1946, it returned to civilian use, with extended railways and repair shops. [17]

Numerous developers from San Francisco, San Jose, and Oakland began building houses in the area in the early 1940s, resulting in developments with such names as Concord Uplands, Concord Vista, Glenbrook Heights, and Holbrook Heights. On January 4, 1949, Mason-McDuffie Real Estate began selling its first houses in a 120-unit development called Maravilla. The two- and three-bedroom houses sold for $10,750, while requiring only $1,075 down. The Berkeley-based firm had constructed numerous housing developments throughout the East Bay and San Francisco but this was its first venture in central Contra Costa County.

Real estate companies realized that veteran families would need housing after the war. They also realized that these veterans had access to low-interest loans and a dependable source of income. Mason-McDuffie had worked with the federal government in building houses for defense workers during the war. At Maravilla, Mason-McDuffie reserved 71 houses for World War II veterans and their families and eliminated down payments and/or closing costs for veteran buyers. [18] Many of the veteran buyers probably were steered to the development by Dr. H. D. Neufeld, a partner in the Maravilla venture, who practiced medicine near the munitions depot in Port Chicago. His patients included veterans residing in Concord looking for housing. [19]

The presence of large numbers of veterans with young families influenced how Mason-McDuffie sold the Maravilla houses. They fashioned a sense of community that would appeal to rootless veterans. Many new residents came from throughout the United States to the Bay Area. They sought to develop a sense of community and those connections originated within the suburbs. Mason-McDuffie advertisements emphasized the existence of a community with full services that appealed to families. Maravilla maps and plans proclaimed it to be a self-contained community. "Nearby is Concord's community Park and Playground . . . Maravilla is but one block from the grammar school, four blocks from churches, six from shopping, theaters, and bus transportation." [20] The community's completeness may have proven especially comforting to

military wives who were new to the area and therefore less certain about
driving to stores in other towns. Mason-McDuffie sold Maravilla as an
instant "community" rather than simply a housing development.

Mason-McDuffie also promoted the Maravilla suburb as a good
investment. Maravilla advertisements noted that the proximity of the
development to San Francisco and Oakland put it "in direct path of
today's metropolitan growth."[21] This message reassured buyers that
house values would remain high or increase as the area grew.[22]

Despite these efforts to provide information about and access to all
needed services, Mason- McDuffie still found it difficult to create a sense
of community among residents in a totally new suburb. The empty
landscape of the new development raised some concerns among the initial
home buyers who longed for neighbors while wondering who might move
in next door. Mason-McDuffie real estate agent Maurice G. Read, who
was also an investor in the Maravilla development, praised a couple for
helping the agent sell the house next door. Read noted that the
Silverfoots "have been our best agents in trying to get the house next door
sold" since they were "anxious to get friendly neighbors."[23]

Mason-McDuffie and Read tried to create the image that Maravilla
was a somewhat exclusive development. The houses in Maravilla were
priced slightly higher than the average tract home. Deeds included racial
covenants excluding non-whites from ownership, although there is no
evidence of prospective minority buyers being interested in the houses.
The moderate prices may have been beyond the financial limits of
minority buyers. Also, minorities faced discrimination from lenders.[24]
Thus, the deed restrictions functioned as symbols of community in the
face of increased regional transiency. The deed restrictions defined
Maravilla residents as like-minded, added a sense of exclusivity, and
united buyers by excluding "outsiders."

Another way McDuffie and Read sought to imply exclusivity was by
forming a homeowner association. Read organized and ran the Maravilla
Homes Association. He was vitally interested in the creation of the
association as a symbol of community and of exclusivity. The association
provided residents the opportunity to get involved in maintaining their
houses' value. Read viewed the association as an important selling point.
He noted that the association would enhance and protect homeowners'
investment, enforce protective covenants, promote community spirit and
activities, and insure stable and attractive neighborhoods.[25]

Increasing metropolitan mobility and rapid construction of housing
and stores in the suburbs made these goals problematic. Predicting a
neighborhood's future was difficult given migration into and out of the
suburbs. Yet Read was attempting to turn a negative into a positive:
buyers could oversee their neighborhood's growth from its inception by
becoming active in the Maravilla Homes Association.

Despite Read's involvement in creating the association, the sparsely attended meetings disappointed him.   To those who did attend the meetings, Read stressed the responsibility individuals had toward being active in solving the problems of their local neighborhoods and community.   Residents learned that participation was necessary to preserve their neighborhoods, but it also provided opportunities for social interaction.   Homeowners associations facilitated the formation of friendships and created a community of neighbors.   In announcing a meeting of the Maravilla Homes Association, Read called the occasion "a social get-together" and "a fine opportunity for you to become better acquainted with your neighbors."[26]

In the Maravilla Homes Association, residents also learned they had a stake in the community and that they should be active in maintaining the value of their investments.   This meant protesting anything that might lower values such as the construction of a factory or low-income housing in the area.   Read solicited suggestions for improving the Maravilla tract and noted, "remember this is your 'town meeting'—come prepared to participate in an interactive and enjoyable evening."[27]

Real estate developers had a vital interest in homeowner associations, which they used to back their claims before local and federal agencies. Housing construction involved constant negotiation between developers, contractors, investors, federal agencies, and local officials.   Developers paid out deposits to the city to ensure that services and roads were constructed according to code.   The city then returned the deposit after the new construction passed inspection.   Builders testified before city councils when complaints arose about the quality of the work performed by contractors hired by the developers.   In one instance, the city council criticized roads built by contractors hired by Mason-McDuffie, and refused to return deposits until workers corrected the problems.   Read insisted that the deposit should be returned because the work was completed.[28]

Over-construction of houses in rural areas caused ecological problems. The new houses were designed to take advantage of the attractive views offered by hillside locations. These locations required that roads be built on hills. Paving hillsides often inhibited natural drainage, which resulted in flooding during winter storms.   Stopping the flooding required new gutters, drains, and culverts, which produced lawsuits as city officials and developers haggled over who was most responsible for correcting these problems.

Developers tried to wiggle out of obligations by blaming their competitors for causing the problems.   One Concord developer argued that the deed restrictions covered in the buying agreements could not be altered to allow the construction of flood prevention structures like a pumping house.[29] Besides local officials, developers also ran into conflicts with federal agencies. The FHA and the VA pressured developers when they received complaints from homeowners about flimsy construction materials or lax design. Developers used homeowner associations to solve problems that buyers encountered before the complaints reached higher authorities. Thus, the homeowner associations helped create, positive outcomes as government officials, homeowners, and developers clashed over various financial issues. The homeowner association was not simply a way of maintaining housing values as is often thought.[30]

THE URBANIZING SUBURB AND THE DECLINE OF COMMUNITY

Individuals involved in homeowner associations felt more connected to local government. Developers used the notion that homeowners had direct access to local government as an essential advantage of living in the suburbs. Unlike the city, where large populations and powerful business interests determined political realities, the suburbs provided individuals with opportunities to make a difference by participating in neighborhood discussions, which directly influenced municipal policy.

This linkage of suburbs and community activism became important as the suburbs underwent rapid growth in the 1960s. Those residents critical of rapid growth increasingly lamented the "decline of community" and the rise of professional experts who, they claimed, subverted the suburb's "traditional" orientation toward family and community. This clash would reach its fullest expression in the 1980s and 1990s.

The concept of "hegemony" suggests that those in control of a society's politics can create a discourse that discourages challenges to the status quo. One way to impose hegemony is through public ceremonies that create or invent traditions that favor the continuation of the dominant class' position in society. Thus, public ceremonies reinforce a dominant group's power by suggesting that present realities are a continuation of long-held traditions.[31]

Developers tried to shape local community ideology. They used homeowner associations to reinforce and maintain a family-oriented community identity. H. D. Neufeld, one of the investors in the Maravilla development, held a contest, in 1945, to pick a motto for Concord. The chosen entries were: "The Bedroom of Contra Costa County" and "Concord: Where Industry Comes Home."[32] Both mottos identified Concord with the single-family house and family, and contrasted the suburb with the city.

The developers and the homeowners' associations promoted and defended the area's family orientation. Early suburbanites wrote the history of their communities in ways that reinforced a family orientation.[33] Concord's historians highlighted the settlement of early white families, beginning with the extended families of the early

Spanish/Mexican land grantees and continuing to the 1960s. This history supported the hegemonic definition of community as family centered begun by Read and various residents.

But by the early 1960s, the community ideal seemed threatened by rapid growth. Concord had a population of 6,973 in 1950 and it grew to 36,208 in 1960. By 1966, it more than doubled to 74,958, and Concord was adding 540 persons per month.[34] Rapid growth created many new problems. One editorial, "Growing Up: The Case of Concord," noted the central issue: rapid growth brought new financial and ecological problems. Development placed new demands on local tax payers for more schools, better flood control, sanitation, and fire and police services.[35] These new pressures required leaders of "vision, dynamism, decisiveness and courage." Leaders believed the public needed to realize that "progress costs money" and should not "obstruct the leaders when they say a step forward is essential."[36]

One area of particular concern was the city's central plaza. While the city's population grew, the central square, called Todos Santos Plaza, had declined. Highways created malls on the suburban fringe, while difficulties with parking discouraged downtown shoppers. Reviving the central plaza area required a new city plan. Some money was available from the federal government, but business leaders asked Concord residents to invest in a new city plan. To fail meant the city would "find itself built around a downtown which produces little public wealth in sales taxes, poor facilities for shoppers and no pride at all in the breasts of the citizens."[37] But could the old values of community-based activism work in such a rapidly changing, complex environment?

Concord's growth also led to a movement by residents to improve the Concord's cultural offerings. In 1967, the city council voted to establish a Cultural Study Committee to assess "the feasibility of adopting a program dedicated to cultural awareness and appreciation in the city." While there were many individuals involved in the arts, the city lacked a performing arts center or an exhibition hall, and culture in the city was not "presently flourishing."[38]

The commission wrestled with whether Concord should aspire to become a regional art center or concentrate on exhibiting local artists. Though they concluded the city should do both, in actuality the report concentrated on the need for a local public arts program. Once again, in the face of rapid population growth, Concord residents used history to maintain its family-focused ethos. Local boosters noted that many "old families in the area own articles that belonged to the original California settlers" and those artifacts could fill a museum and demonstrate the family history of the city. They also noted the many local artists with talents who needed a place to display those talents.[39] Thus exhibiting local family history was deemed more important than luring outsiders to the community.

This new interest in the suburb's cultural base reflected a desire to maintain a sense of community in the face of rapid growth. Concord was beginning to attract shoppers from throughout the region. Sunvalley Mall, which opened in summer 1967, was billed as the world's largest climate controlled shopping center. Sunvalley Mall was located alongside a major freeway that linked Concord, Walnut Creek, Oakland, and San Francisco. The mall initially housed 55 stores, including Sears, Macy's, and J. C. Penney's. By 1987, the mall had expanded to 165 stores and brought in $3 million in annual tax revenues, the largest single contributor to the city budget.[40] In 1965, Systron-Donnor Corp., a scientific research firm, moved from Berkeley to Concord, and in 1970, Standard Oil of California moved its credit card processing offices to the suburb.[41]

While the new firms' revenues helped offset homeowners' tax increases, the money also allowed Concord to project a new cosmopolitanism to which it could not previously aspire. In the late 1960s, car dealer Carl Jefferson founded a summer music festival, which became an annual event that led to the construction of an outdoor pavilion. The 8,000-seat Concord Pavilion was financed through city bonds and a 1973 joint powers agreement between Concord and the Mount Diablo Unified School District. The donation of 122 acres by real estate developer Ken Hofmann enabled the city to afford the $4.5 million structure. Completed in 1975, the Concord Pavilion was an open-air amphitheater designed by the renowned architect Frank O. Gehry. The annual Concord Jazz Festival gave Concord local, regional, and national recognition.[42]

Concord's growth by 1970 led some to refer to Concord as a city rather than a suburb. In 1968, Mayor Warren Boggess noted that it was "not only Concord's 100th Anniversary" but also "the year when [Concord] ceased to be a mere suburb of Oakland and San Francisco and truly came of age as a city."[43]

Concord's growth into a city was not celebrated by everyone. Some residents recalled the early suburb's family-centered identity and continued to support that orientation. For example, during its centennial celebration, community leaders recognized local individuals for their length of residency in the town. Among celebrants receiving awards was a druggist who owned the oldest Concord business (41 years). Others received awards for being the oldest descendent of original town founders, as well as for longest length of service in various capacities (fire chief, school teacher, elected official).

The celebration was dubbed "Pioneer Day" and reflected worries over the suburb's growth. The festivities were held in the old downtown, an area left largely unchanged by the suburban development taking place in the outskirts. Those honored descended from the old Californio families who recalled the town's origins as a Spanish settlement. The mayor renamed the central square "Todos Santos Plaza," the Spanish name for the early community. During the event, several "old-timers played a local history trivia game.[44] Highlighting those individuals active in the community's founding and growth reinforced an older family-centered suburban identity.

The celebration of elderly residents who had run the town in the past indicated how much the city had changed. By the 1970s, growth required that Concord consult with professionals to deal with the problems of expansion. Long-time residents no longer possessed the skills needed to plan the growing community's future. Local government was hampered because it still reflected the parochial days when devoted citizens participated in public service. The city needed technically trained experts to grapple with social and economic problems facing a modern city.[45]

The new planners pushed for greater efforts to lure outsiders into the downtown to stem its economic stagnation. A 1963 study concluded that Central Concord was in decline due to competition from surrounding shopping centers. The plaza was compact and lacked sufficient parking. New stores preferred the more spacious accommodations located along the freeways with abundant parking and direct access to distant points in the Bay Area. The report argued that all Concord residents needed to support the redevelopment of downtown. Maintaining the central area was important since loss of business would diminish tax revenues and lead to higher homeowner taxes. A vacant downtown would cause the city's image as a desirable residential area to decline, which would diminish housing values. "Few residents can avoid Central Concord on their daily trips to work, to shop, or to school. If community pride and identity are to be maintained, Central Concord must match the community's estimate of itself."[46]

Despite this warning, a study in 1970 indicated that downtown's decline had continued. A special report on Todos Santos Plaza concluded that the area was stagnating. "A profound change is required to reverse this condition." Yet the plaza continued to serve local patrons very well. Elderly residents who had resided in the area for years patronized the shopping district, which provided a variety of stores in a compact area. But the study noted that the elderly residents had "a lower demand for consumer goods and services." Therefore the key to redevelopment of downtown, the study concluded, was to lure new shoppers into the plaza area who would be more willing to buy higher priced goods.[47] Another planning study recommended for the downtown area a regional hotel and convention center, and a regional apartment village designed for "single adults, and childless couples of middle- and upper-middle income." The village "would possess a sophisticated urbane character, spirit, and amenities," and ideally would be "clustered around common greens or squares, neighborhood shops, excellent restaurants."[48]

San Francisco was the model for Concord's new downtown plan. In arguing for an upscale image that would attract young professionals, the 1968 study noted that "San Francisco is a world-famed 'walking city' despite rugged terrain, traffic congestion, and disagreeable weather. People enjoy exploring the city on foot because San Francisco is urbane, scenic, cosmopolitan, intimate, personal and charming." Concord needed to use "imagination and design" to create a similarly "urban environment" that was "more than functional," but that would attract people to the city "for the pleasure of it, rather than only on shopping errands."[49] The physical nature of exploring a city on foot clearly indicated a preference for young urban explorers to replace the senior citizens that presently resided in and near the downtown.

The conflict over whether the downtown should serve local residents or regional visitors was not new. The city had proposed a major overhaul of the plaza's green space in 1960. After seeing the plans, some residents criticized officials for being primarily interested in luring outside shoppers into the stores surrounding the plaza rather then meeting the needs of local recreational users.[50] Thus, in both art and architecture, a division grew up between those seeking to serve local residents and those envisioning the city as a regional center.

THE SPANISH MYTH AND DOWNTOWN CONCORD

While the city grew rapidly in the 1970s, the downtown remained largely untouched. The few new businesses that had relocated there conformed to Concord's traditional suburban image by adopting Spanish mission revival architecture. Todos Santos Plaza continued to serve mostly local residents.

The 1970s did see the proliferation of the use of Spanish architecture and references to the community's early Hispanic settlers. Concord business and government officials began utilizing the Spanish myth to distinguish Concord from the other suburbs in the area.[51] They felt Spanish architecture would provide Concord with an interesting history that, because of its familiarity to Bay Area residents, might also serve to attract visitors from all parts of the region. The myth is ubiquitous in the Bay Area where Spanish names identified mountains, streets, stores, suburbs, cities, famous families, historic homes, parks, and hospitals. Red tile roofs, colorful mosaic walls, adobe houses, and elaborate fountains and gardens represented the historic presence of the Spanish in the area.[52]

The myth was not new. Developers helped bring the myth to Concord by building new houses and shopping areas with Spanish architecture. In 1948, H. D. Neufeld had purchased an old adobe house and remodeled it into a restaurant, hoping the historic structure would lure other businesses to the area.[53] In the 1960s, the myth became the major cultural theme in downtown. During the 1968 anniversary celebration the central plaza was renamed "Todos Santos Plaza" and became the site for an annual downtown fiesta that included mariachis, crafts, food, and antiques.[54]

Many groups supported the Spanish myth. References to the early Hispanic families reaffirmed the suburb's family-centered identity. Nostalgia for the area's rural past also motivated the use of the Spanish myth. The myth particularly resonated among long-time residents, like Ruth Galindo, who helped found the Concord Historical Society in 1971. Galindo traced her family history back six generations to the early Spanish-Mexican settlers of California.[55]

Not just older residents, but many businesses adopted the myth hoping to stimulate the downtown economy. The myth presented a historic landscape that many outside Concord were familiar with. The myth allowed commercialization to proceed without challenging the family-centered suburban image of the old downtown.

The use of the myth also helped obscure the fact that new commercial chains were supplanting locally owned establishments. Locally owned banks had previously been a great source of community pride. The community held bankers in high esteem. But the rise of large banking chains eliminated any special local affection for banks. In 1977, Associated Bank, a statewide chain, purchased and refurbished the old adobe formerly owned by Neufeld. In its advertisements, the bank used the myth to attach itself to the community. One advertisement pictured Salvador Pacheco (Don Salvio's son) and his family, with two horses, in front of the adobe. The advertisement noted that the Pacheco family had planted trees on the site that still stood, and that the bank would preserve for the community, along with the adobe itself. The picture of Don Salvio suggested the bewildering impact on the Californios of the transition to Anglo rule. Long-time Concord residents experienced a similar sense of loss in the transformation of their rural community into a city. The advertisement implied that the new bank chain would benefit Concord by preserving the community's identity and history.

The bank used the myth not to criticize suburbia but to celebrate Concord as a good place for families. The advertisement referred to the "home" of Don Salvio. Just as the Salvios built a home in Concord, the advertisement indicated that Associated Bank made it possible for families to buy houses. The advertisement linked the bank to the city's development. The "home" of Don Salvio referred to a community of home owners who utilized mortgages to finance their movement to the suburbs.

References to the Spanish past gave the remaining Hispanic descendants special status as living representatives of the community's history.[56] Bank officials consulted local resident expert and relative of Don Salvio and Californio descendent Ruth Galindo in its retelling of the community's history.   Galindo became the most recognized expert of local history.   She taught Spanish in Concord high schools and consulted on many historical projects including preservation, tours, and new historic landmarks. She owned a house near Todos Santos Plaza and she exhibited old photographs of the extended Galindo clan, and period furniture. Without children to carry forward the family name, her home, which she deeded to the city upon her death, was to be transformed into a local history museum.[57]   The myth satisfied both businesses and residents by maintaining a sense of community history while allowing development to proceed.

By 1980, the city's population had reached 102,000.   Increased traffic and lengthened commutes between the suburbs and San Francisco and Oakland, and new communication technologies made Concord more viable as a business location.[58]   Concord's downtown began attracting multinational corporations because of its BART station, its freeway access, and its available work force.   Bank of America and Wells Fargo Bank built new office complexes near the BART station and the plaza. Chevron and Shell expanded the processing of credit card accounts. Though workers took BART from throughout the Bay Area to Concord, few lived in the city and fewer stayed after work hours to shop or eat in the downtown area.   These were the young urban professionals whom city planners since the 1960s had hoped to entice to revive the downtown's economy. Getting them to settle and to spend money in the city became the goal of city leaders.[59]

THE SPIRIT POLES CONTROVERSY

In the 1980s, growing numbers of commuters from throughout the Bay Area worked in Concord, including many professionals.   Their presence encouraged Concord leaders to create a sophisticated urban image for the city so that more commuters would stay in the downtown after work hours to eat, drink, and shop.   Concord's nearby suburban rival, Walnut Creek, had successfully used public art to stimulate its economy.   Walnut Creek's extensive public art program had increased local appreciation for art and brought support for cultural events culminating with the construction of a regional performing arts center.[60]

The concern that Concord lacked cultural programming was not new. In the late 1960s, the city formed an arts committee that after comparing Concord to other towns of comparable size concluded that "culture in Concord is not presently flourishing." Local artists needed the funding and the facilities to display their talents.   The committee established a commission to study ways to get more residents involved in supporting local artists. The majority of the commission was composed of local residents. Thus, during this period, city leaders primarily saw the arts as something produced by and for locals, not a way of attracting outsiders into the community.[61]

By the 1980s, the perspective on art in Concord had changed. Increasingly, the city became more aware that art could enhance Concord's regional image. "People tend to look down their noses at us," one city council member complained in 1988. Even worse, outsiders possessed a "very negative" image of Concord residents as "blue collar workers and uneducated people."[62] A public arts program would reverse Concord's image as a cultureless suburb.

In 1985, the city council adopted an Art in Public Places (AIPP) ordinance requiring developers of new downtown office structures to contribute one-half percent of their construction budget into a fund administered by the city's Redevelopment Agency that supported public art.[63] This fund paid for the Concord Heritage Gateway, a project to beautify nine boulevards leading into downtown Concord. The plan called for each boulevard median to feature art that represented a different phase of Concord's history.

One part of the Concord Heritage Gateway was the conversion of five medians on Concord Avenue in the heart of downtown into public art sights. The Concord Redevelopment Agency, working with the city's art commission, and a National Endowment for the Arts jury, held a competition in 1986 and the city council selected a design submitted by Ohio artist Gary Rieveschl. Rieveschl collaborated with local landscape architect Michael Fotheringham and produced what the local papers would dub the "Spirit Poles." The public viewed plans for the project at two town meetings in 1986, and in 1987 a model appeared at the city's Fall Fest celebration where 200 signed a sheet supporting the project.[64] City visual arts administrator Hawley Holmes showed the plans to numerous civic clubs. The city arts commission voted unanimously for the project. Some residents, however, did write in during a community survey and criticized the sculpture for being cold and stark. Nevertheless, in 1988 the city council approved the project by a 3-2 vote. Construction began in June 1989, and the project was completed in November 1989.[65]

The work stretched along the Concord Avenue median for five city blocks (Photo 6). The first island, entitled "the Ancients," contained an oak tree symbolizing the original inhabitants of the area, the Ohlone Indians, and their "community spirit of mutual nourishment and protection." The second island, entitled "the Settlers," featured a small orchard of flowering trees representing the first Hispanic settlers who founded the town of Todos Santos. The third island, entitled "the Agrarians," represented the advent of modern agriculture, and featured a formal garden with hedges and flowers.[66]

The final two islands were the most controversial. They contained the abstract sculpture composed of 91 aluminum poles with pointed tips, ranging from 6 to 50 feet in length. In the first island, entitled "The Advent of Modern Technology," the poles stood at various heights and angles to suggest cycles of technological growth. The final island, called "The Age of Information," contains a double line of angled poles suggesting "our increasing interdependence in an electronic age of digitalized information." The poles increased in length as one traveled

Photo 6.
"Spirit Poles," Downtown Concord, 1998

toward the city center.[67] A walkway meandered through the poles to a "Spirit Place" where residents could ponder the community's evolution from an Ohlone Indian settlement into a bustling city, and "reaffirm our respectful responsibility to this land our children will inherit."[68]

The entire project cost $400,000. After completion, Concord residents wrote letters to the *Contra Costa Times* ridiculing the sculpture as ugly and waste of money. They claimed sculpture was threatening and that it scared drivers who feared the poles would fall on their cars during an earthquake. The poles looked like missiles, which some found appropriate given the existence nearby of the Concord Naval Weapons Station where ammunition was shipped to the U.S. armed forces during overseas conflicts. Residents derogatorily referred to the poles as knitting needles, rockets, chop sticks, and shish kebab skewers.

The clamor against the Spirit Poles coincided with several other controversies that resulted in the ouster from office of Mayor June Bulman and three other city council members. The city council had passed a controversial law prohibiting discrimination against people with AIDS. Local fundamentalist preacher Rev. Lloyd Mashore organized opposition to those city council members who supported the sculpture and the AIDS anti-discrimination ordinance, and he launched a drive to repeal the ordinance.[69]

The backlash culminated with the election in November of 1989 of a conservative city council that included Mashore and effected the repeal of the AIDS anti-discrimination ordinance. The council selected Byron Campbell, a Spirit Poles opponent, as mayor. Campbell immediately called for removal of the sculpture, but found that the city would face a legal challenge from the artist. Because of the critical reaction to the sculpture and the repeal of the AIDS anti-discrimination ordinance, Concord became known in the Bay Area as the northern California counterpoint of sunny and conservative Orange County.[70]

This new conservative backlash reflected a resistance to the suburb's urbanization. The Spirit Poles supporters believed its opponents were resisting the inevitability of local change. "A lot of people feel that they don't want to give up on that vision of the barbecue or the bandstand in the park." Yet Concord was no longer a small town as as it had been in the 1950s and 1960s. Progressive residents felt Concord should accept its urban identity. "Concord is not a horse and buggy town anymore." The city had modern high rises and the Spirit Poles "enhances the new image of our city as an up-to-date, growing metropolis."[71] Another supporter felt the poles fit because Concord "is rapidly shifting its identity from a sleepy rural village to residential suburb to high-rise urban area where people 'come' to work."[72]

Part of urbanization meant increased dependence on experts. City planners and other government officials were increasingly hired from outside communities. Critics of the Spirit Poles believed that town leaders who supported the sculpture condescended to the public. Because the sculpture was abstract and therefore its meaning was not readily apparent, outside experts with training in art had to interpret the work for the residents. Spirit Poles critics were angered by "the attitude by those who selected and approved the project that they are 'experts' who know more about art than the rest of us. Therefore we should bow to their expertise and accept whatever is created."[73] Yet some admitted that the poles were erected because few had attended the open hearings and that the sculpture had the positive impact of getting more residents active in local politics.

The major criticism of the Spirit Poles was that it did not reflect "Concord's spirit."[74] Critics viewed the poles as representing big city values, which Concord did not wish to emulate. The art was deemed more suitable for a big city. One resident noted, "I wonder what the response to this art would be if it were located in a large city like L.A. or New York?"[75] Another resident suggested that the designers take the poles "right back to New York where they would fit perfectly and give the money back to Concord."[76] Another resident said, "change is one thing. But this is something you might see in New York or San Francisco. It is too far out for Concord."[77] In a survey of public opinion about the sculpture, one respondent argued that "Concord should not look like a city metropolis. Most natives live here for the rural atmosphere and are disappointed in the urban growth."[78] One resident suggested Spirit Poles would be more appropriately located between the modern Bank of America and Wells Fargo Bank office buildings.[79]

In referencing Indian spirituality and culture, the Spirit Poles implied a direct criticism of suburbia's materialism and individualism. Thus the sculpture, which city officials endorsed as a way to overcome Concord's small-town image, exhibited stereotypical thinking about Concord's suburban history. One supporter of the Spirit Poles noted that "suburban life is a rejection of community." This supporter insisted that those who criticized the Spirit Poles were not "protecting a community vision, but protecting the absence of a community vision."[80] In celebrating the suburb's newfound urban sophistication, the sculpture came under fire for ridiculing its suburban community values.

By emphasizing the community's multicultural past, the sculpture indirectly criticized the celebration of Concord's "Spanish" heritage and the Spanish myth that was such an important part of the community's official memory. This particularly galled some residents since the Spirit Poles was located in the heart of the downtown where the Spanish myth so strongly prevailed. One critic noted that he was "proud of Concord and what good taste they showed in the past—even preserved those beautiful old Victorian style homes, the Salvio Pacheco Square, built in such beautiful taste—then such an ugly thing right in Old Town Concord. Why is the population of Concord not being asked to decide what is going up in Concord?"[81] Others noted the poles "don't match the downtown" and they "appear contradictory" to the appearance of the "historical Spanish architecture—exemplified by Salvio Pacheco Square"[82] One believed that "the architecture of the new and remodeled buildings in downtown Concord are in a beautiful Spanish motif. Where is the connection with the long aluminum nails sticking up in the air?"[83]

Sculpture critics also realized that despite the multicultural cast of the Spirit Poles, public art was part of an attempt to increase commercial activity in downtown Concord. Residents believed that the aggressively cold sculpture would actually scare away visitors. Supporters had felt the project would give Concord an upscale image. Some continued to believe that. One supporter wrote, "Congratulations to the city of Concord on making a dynamic artistic statement. The Heritage Gateway shows the forward-thinking spirit of the city. The new Bank of America building and all of the other modern structures now have an appropriate introduction to the motorists approaching the city."[84] Thus, the conflict over the Spirit Poles pitted local residents against efforts to appeal to younger professional newcomers. The city's public art committee noted that "you can never please everyone." Rather, the conflict indicated the conflict in trying to please the resident and pleasing the "newcomer or visitor to the city, because the appearance and image of the city is important."[85]

The Spirit Poles bore the brunt of local concerns over the changes taking place in the community. The relocation of offices and firms brought in highly trained professionals whom Concord leaders were trying to attract as visitors, workers, and permanent residents. These leaders had failed, said one critic, to take into account Concord's "blue-collar and middle-class roots" when deciding on the public art. The reaction against the Spirit Poles was an attempt by locals to withstand the urbanization of the suburb.

TODOS SANTOS PLAZA

Simultaneously with the Spirit Poles debacle, there occurred a controversy over the refurbishment of Concord's old plaza. Given to the city in 1868 by town founder Don Salvio Pacheco, the plaza was in the heart of downtown, a block away from the Spirit Poles. Todos Santos Plaza remained largely unchanged until 1950. It included trees, a bandstand, and a dance platform surrounded by small locally owned shops. In 1912, a Carnegie Library was built and it was torn down in 1957. Prior to the 1950s, the plaza's most notable feature was its wisteria that clung to the largest redwood pergola on the West Coast. Before removing the pergola for child safety reasons, the town had sponsored an annual wisteria festival.[86]

In 1960, plans for another remodeling encountered resistance from recreational users who claimed that the plaza should not just be considered "a shopper's mall" for the surrounding businesses. Concord had few other public parks, which made the plaza important for recreation. Yet the plans ignored the interests of local residents.[87]

But as Concord urbanized, the plaza became a place to stage events to draw shoppers. In the 1970s, an annual "Black Bart Days" festival was held in the plaza, which included crafts, food, antiques, and mariachis.[88] City leaders began to remodel the plaza in 1982 when a new office and retail building was erected in "early California" style with a red-tile roof, adobe walls, a colonnade, wrought iron railing, mosaics, and a fountain. The project originally featured 79 condominiums but lack of financing forced their elimination.[89] The building was located alongside the grassy plaza.

The next step involved redesigning the plaza itself. The city sponsored a design contest in 1988 and a jury of architects, artists, a museum director, and representatives from the community's art committee selected the plan by San Francisco architects Peter Walker and Martha Schwartz, which featured crossing pathways of various materials to encourage strolling through the park to the surrounding shops, a stage, and a play area. The design also featured playground equipment made of several structures representing Concord's history, including the foundation from an adobe and ranch home with an unfinished wooden staircase. The playground equipment included a bronze mission chair, and most controversially, a bronze "suburban barcalounger" symbolizing the town's growth during the Spanish era and the rise of suburbia. Finally, a wisteria-covered lattice completed the references to Concord's history.[90]

The design received very mixed reviews. One supporter called Todos Santos Plaza "a nice little park but it's just a park. It doesn't go with the rest of the city." Instead, Concord "should have a park that makes a statement, so when you drive past and (you say) 'Look at that.'" He supported the redesigned plaza, which would draw national attention to the city. Other supporters anticipated the design winning national public design contests.[91]

Yet some residents saw the redesigned plaza as smacking of intellectual elitism. Ruth Galindo proclaimed, "I am not sure that Concord is a sophisticated enough city to interpret some of (the design's) aspects." Galindo stated that she "went by there today and it looks so pretty and tranquil. I'd hate to see it disturbed to the extent they want to. It's a little space and it shouldn't be jammed with ideas."[92]

Opponents formed a group called "Friends of Todos Santos Plaza" and claimed it had not been notified of the public hearings where the committee considered the plan.   "What has taken place is not due process," complained a city council member.[93]   Another resident suggested that while the design sounded "fine on paper I don't think the average person walking through the park is going to be able to grasp what they [the designers] are attempting to do."[94]   Other critics were concerned with the city's urbanization.   One observer believed the sculptures would entice "marker toting graffiti vandals" and could offer hiding places for muggers.[95]

The bronze barcalounger raised eyebrows. For some the recliner was a whimsical modern sculpture suggesting simultaneously a new urban sophistication and a disdain for what the chair symbolized: suburban parochialism.   The recliner was a master stroke at once celebrating a newfound urbanity evidenced in the embracing of modern art, while indicating how far Concord had progressed from its days as a bedroom suburb.

Yet the chair became a focal point of contention deemed by many as too avant-garde for Concord. It did not fit the community's support for a family-oriented image. It smacked of an urbanity that was better suited to bigger cities. The designers agreed to "reupholster" the barcalounger and transform it into a mission chair.[96] Yet critics remained opposed to any modern sculpture, particularly after the Spirit Poles controversy. Newly elected mayor, Byron Campbell, was also a member of Friends of Todos Santos Plaza. He supported a design that maintained Concord's small-town feel. "Concord lacks a set of traditional values and the park should reflect [traditional] values," stated Campbell, "not some cumulative history and representational art."[97]

The criticism eventually led the Concord city council to scuttle the winning design and vote to implement a very subdued plaza renovation that lacked the barcalounger or any other modern sculpture (Photo 7). The plaza continued to represent the traditional view of the community's "Spanish" history by including plaques honoring the Salvios and the Pachecos (Photo 8).

The fallout caused by the Spirit Poles and the plaza renovation highlighted growing concerns over the urbanization of Concord. With the rise of high-rise office buildings downtown, some older residents claimed the plaza as a space for the exhibition of traditional family-centered, suburban values and of history as embodied in the Spanish myth. For these older residents, the modern high-rises, the Spirit Poles, and the Todos Santos Plaza redesign suggested that the city was catering to outsiders. The "Spanish" architecture became part of their effort to preserve Concord's suburban culture. Conversely, those who supported modern public art insisted that Concord had changed. It was no longer a sleepy suburban town, and its residents would be better served to accept the changes. But for older residents, the changes made them more adamant that the plaza remain an oasis of the community's traditional family-centered ideals.

Urbanization both undermined and strengthened the community's ties to the early Spanish settlers. The money that downtown developers paid into the AIPP fund produced the Spirit Poles, which celebrated cultural diversity and modern art, particularly the early Native American inhabitants. Urbanization, however, also increased nostalgia for Concord's supposed Spanish roots. In 1993, the city's *Concord Transcript* published a Centennial Edition. The front page included a story on Ruth Galindo, which described her as "the personification of old Spanish California."[98] A recent historical brochure includes Galindo's house, built in 1856, and the statement that "few cities in California can boast that a direct descendant of its founder still resides within the city limits in the original family home."[99] As the high-rises proliferated, Concord residents reflected on its small-town past, which they equated with the city's older residents like Galindo and the early Spanish families.

Old-timers like Galindo tried to use the Spanish myth to maintain some modicum of influence over local development. The city council in 1987 empowered Ruth Galindo, based on her illustrious family past, to nominate buildings suitable for historical preservation.[100] By fighting to

Photo 7.
Todos Santos Plaza, Concord, 1998

preserve the Spanish myth, Galindo became an activist for resident participation in city planning. She criticized the plans for the new plaza on several occasions, and she campaigned for a height limitation on downtown structures. She argued that the new buildings crowded her old Victorian home located near downtown, which she planned on bequeathing for a city museum. The clapboard house sits today in the middle of the bustling downtown. Surrounded by shade trees, the structure is nearly invisible from the street. It serves as a good symbol of local resistance to urbanization. In 1987, the city council adopted a two-story height limit on new buildings slated for construction near the house.[101]   Galindo's family home recalled the town's origins as a residential suburb.

Concord's urbanization encouraged Ruth Galindo to cling to her ethnic identity in order to maintain influence over local affairs. She, like many other Concord residents, believed that the new high-rises had undermined the town's suburban identity. The Spirit Poles indicated the arrival of a new urban culture that emphasized cultural pluralism, change, and acceptance of differences over a suburban culture that stressed community consensus and local traditions. Galindo, her house, and

Photo 8.
Historic Plaques, Todos Santos Plaza, Concord, 1998

Todos Santos Plaza became the last holdouts against the urbanization of the suburb.

CONCLUSION

By the 1990s, growing numbers of younger residents, gays, Asians, blacks, and Mexicans lived or worked in Concord. The increased presence of these groups called into question the Spanish myth. That the Spanish myth would no longer be the only perspective on the community's history was made evident following the opening of the remodeled Todos Santos Plaza. A public celebration of the Mexican holiday, Cinco de Mayo, drew an unexpectedly large crowd of 8,000, including numerous Latinos. After the event, a city official criticized the celebrants for trampling flower beds, damaging the new sod, and littering the park.[102] Mexican American Roberto Castellon, publisher of a Spanish language newspaper, angrily refuted the charges. "I spent 28 years in the Army, two years in Vietnam, 31 days in the hospital and I am not going to stand for this. The Hispanic community is not going to stand for this."[103] The Cinco de Mayo event indicated that the community's changing demographics would challenge the Spanish myth. The celebration of a Mexican holiday had turned out thousands. No longer would the Spanish myth, which celebrated white European exploration and conquest, be the only perspective on local history. No longer would the Californio descendants have unchallenged control of the Spanish myth. Residents would ask about Ohlone Indian, Mexican, and Asian history, rather than simply accept the interpretations given by the older residents.

Rapid growth in San Jose and Concord created community identity crises, which produced conflicts over how to represent local history. Yet conflicts arose not only because of increased ethnic and racial diversity within these cities. For years, San Jose and Concord had struggled with the effects of urbanization produced by new regional connections. Concord grew up after World War II as a typical suburban community. Developers put in place homeowner associations that encouraged residents to get involved in community affairs. Concord residents embraced their community's identity as a bedroom suburb that supported family life. The Spanish myth fit that identity and so naturally was important to popular historical memory. Concord local historians celebrated the Californios for their large families, their family orientation, and their honorable character.

However, by the 1970s rapid growth undermined a sense of community. Professional planners and politicians played increasingly important roles. BART's opening in 1976 led to the urbanization of the downtown. Outsiders began commuting to Concord. The Spirit Poles and the Todos Santos Plaza redesign represented attempts by local leaders to address the community's changing demographics, which included more young single professionals and minorities. City officials attempted to cater to the visitors and lure more into their downtown districts by presenting an urbanized culture that welcomed diverse newcomers.

Local residents, however, criticized the urbanization of the suburb, which they believed undermined family traditions. They saw suburban culture as supportive of families while the Spirit Poles and the plan for the remodeled Todos Santos Plaza both portrayed suburban culture as parochial. While they could not stop the high-rises, they could stop the art. But their victory would be short-lived. The Cinco de Mayo controversy indicated that the community's history would have to be revised to include diverse newcomers who would soon wield more power.

Many see the culture wars as the result of deep fissures in American society. Often, however, cultural debates result from the stresses of communities undergoing rapid urban change. By the 1970s, suburbs like Concord were becoming more independent of cities. As Concord began to compete with cities and other suburbs like Walnut Creek for economic and cultural power some leaders looked to cosmopolitanize the suburb. Older residents saw such efforts as undermining its original identity as a family-based residential community. Thus the battles over the Spirit Poles and Todos Santos Plaza were part of a necessary debate about the community's past, present, and future values and identity.

NOTES

1.   California Fair Employment and Housing Commission, *Public Hearing on Racial and Ethnic Discrimination, Conflict, and Violence in Central Contra Costa County* (San Francisco, 1986), 12.

2.   See Robert Fishman, "America's New City," *Wilson Quarterly* 14, no. 1 (Winter 1990): 24–55; Robert Geddes, "Metropolis Unbound," *The American Prospect* 35 (Novemeber-December 1997): 40–46.

3.   See Rob Kling, Spencer Olin, and Mark Poster, eds., *Postsuburban California: The Transformation of Orange County Since World War II* (Berkeley, 1991); Joel Garreau, *Edge City: Life on the New Frontier* (New York, 1991); Louis H. Masotti and Jeffrey K. Hadden, eds., *The Urbanization of the Suburbs* (Beverly Hills, 1973); Peter O. Muller, *The Outer City: Geographical Consequences of the Urbanization of the Suburbs* (Washington D.C., 1976); William Sharpe and Leonard Wallock, "Bold New City or Built-Up 'Burb': Redefining Contemporary Suburbia," *American Quarterly* 46, no. 1 (March 1994): 1–30; Thomas M. Stanback, Jr., *The New Suburbanization: Challenge to the Central City* (Boulder, 1991).

4.   On the role of art in producing the "symbolic economy" or the upscale image so sought after by urban leaders today, see Sharon Zukin, *The Cultures of Cities* (Cambridge, 1995).

5.   See Robert Fisher, *Let the People Decide: Neighborhood Organizing in America*

(Boston, 1984).

6.   Steven C. Dubin, *Arresting Images: Impolitic Art and Uncivil Actions* (New York, 1992).

7.   Erika Doss, *Spirit Poles and Flying Pigs: Public Art and Cultural Democracy in American Communities* (Washington D.C., 1995), 13–34; Ralph Reed, *Active Faith: How Christians are Changing the Soul of American Politics* (New York, 1996), 133.

8.   James Davison Hunter, *Culture Wars: The Struggle to Define America* (New York, 1991), 231–249.

9.   Rosalyn Deutsche, "Urban Development: Public Art in New York City," *October* 47 (Winter 1988): 3–52.

10.   Doss, *Spirit Poles and Flying Pigs*, 21.

11.   Sharon Zukin, "Space and Symbols in an Age of Decline," in Anthony D. King, ed., *Re-Presenting the City: Ethnicity, Capital, and Culture in the 21st Century Metropolis* (New York, 1996), 44.

12.   See George Emanuels, *California's Contra Costa County: An Illustrated History* (Fresno, 1986); Mae Fisher Purcell, *History of Contra Costa County* (Berkeley, 1940).

13.   William Chapin, *The Suburbs of San Francisco* (San Francisco, 1969), 61.

14.   Purcell, *History of Contra Costa County*.

15.   "Concord in the Town of Todos Santos," The History of Concord Research Project (Mt. Diablo School District Summer School, Constra Costa Historical Society, 1967).

16.   R. N. Burgess, *Mount Diablo Estate, The Home and the Club* (San Francisco, n.d.), 16.

17.   Edna May Andrews, *History of Concord: Its Progress and Promise* (Concord, 1986), 168.

18.   Mason McDuffie Company Papers (MMCOP), carton 19 folder 26.

19.   On Neufeld, see Andrews, *History of Concord*, 145.

20.   MMCOP, carton 15 folder 19.

21.   MMCOP, carton 15 folder 12.

22.   MMCOP, carton 15 folder 11.

23.   MMCOP, carton 20 folder 18.

24.   Marc A. Weiss, *The Rise of the Community Builders* (New York, 1987), 68–72.

25.   MMCOP, carton 20 folder 17.

26.   Correspondence from Maurice G. Read to Maravilla Homes Association, February 3, 1949, MMCOP, carton 20 folder 17.

27.   Ibid.

28.   *Concord Transcript*, July 16, 1949.

29.   April 12, 1948, MMCOP, carton 19 folder 40.

30.   For an excellent overview of the topic, see Evan McKenzie, *Privatopia: Homeonwer Associations and the Rise of Residential Private Government* (New Haven, 1994).

31.   On hegemony, see T. Jackson Lears, "The Concept of Cultural Hegemony: Problems and Possibilities," *American Historical Review* 90 (June 1985): 567–593. On public memory see Iwona Irwin-Zarecka, *Frames of Remembrance: The Dynamics of Collective Memory* (New Brunswick, 1994).

32.   "Concord in the Town of Todos Santos."

33.   See Leonora Galindo Fink, *The Pachecos and Galindos: Founding Families of Central Contra Costa County* (Concord, 1957); Leonora Galindo Fink, ed., *The Founders of Todos Santos* (Pleasant Hill, 1963); Andrews, *History of Concord*, 26.

34.   Andrews, *History of Concord*, 99.

35.   *Contra Costa Times*, December 8, 1961.

36.   Ibid.

37.   Ibid.

38.   "Report of the Cultural Study Committee to the City Council of the City of

Concord" (Contra Costa County, California, March 10, 1969), 91.

39. *Contra Costa Times*, May 3, 1964.

40. *Contra Costa Times*, August 7, 1987; *Concord Life* (December 1984): 28–29. On the early history of Bay Area shopping malls, see Warren R. Harris, "Shopping Center Development in the San Francisco Bay Area" (master's thesis, University of California-Berkeley, 1952).

41. Andrews, *History of Concord*, 109–112.

42. *Contra Costa Times*, October 24, 1995; Oakland Tribune, May 16, 1975.

43. *City of Concord Newslette*, September 1968, 1.

44. *Concord Transcript*, September 30, 1968.

45. *Contra Costa Times*, December 5, 1961.

46. *Central Concord Development Plan By Livingston and Blayney Prepared for the City of Concord* (San Francisco, 1963), 1.

47. Concord City Planning Department, *Concord Central Area Plan: Preliminary Economic Study* (Concord, 1970).

48. City of Concord Planing Department, *West Concord Development Plan: An Amendment to the Concord General Plan* (Concord, September 10, 1968), 18.

49. *West Concord Development Plan*, 13–14.

50. *Contra Costa Times*, September 25, 1960.

51. On tourism, see Martha K. Norkunas, *The Politics of Public Memory: Tourism, History, and Ethnicity in Monterey, California* (Albany, 1993); Susan Porter Benson, Stephen Brier, and Roy Rosenzweig, eds., *Presenting the Past: Essays on History and the Public* (Philadelphia, 1986); and Colin Michael Hall, Tourism and Politics: Policy, Power and Place (Chichester, England, 1994).

52. David Lowenthal notes the inevitable similarities of historical shopping districts, like Ghiradelli Square, Quincy Market, and Covent Garden, which reassure the tourist audience through today's "standard display and restoration practices." See Lowenthal, *The Past Is a Foreign Country* (New York, 1985), 351.

53. *Concord Gazette*, July 13, 1948.

54. Andrews, *History of Concord*, 184.

55. Interview with Ruth Galindo by the author, July 31, 1995.

56. Lowenthal, *The Past Is a Foreign Country*, 332.

57. *Concord Transcript*, November 11, 1993.

58. See John R. Borchert, "Futures of American Cities," in John Fraser Hart, ed., *Our Changing Cities* (Baltimore, 1991), 218–250.

59. *Contra Costa Times*, October 28, 1988.

60. Walnut Creek Civic Arts Commission, The Decade Ahead–Civic Arts Ten-Year Plan, 1986-1996: Prepared for the Walnut Creek City Council (Walnut Creek, 1986); George Emanuels, *Walnut Creek: Arroyo de las Nueces* (Walnut Creek, 1984).

61. Concord City Council, *Report of the Cultural Study Committee to the City Concord, County of Contra Costa, State of California* (Concord, 1969).

62. *Contra Costa Times*, October 28, 1988.

63. "The Concord Heritage Gateway, City of Concord Begins New Era in Public Art" (typewritten document, n.d., in possession of author).

64. *Contra Costa Times*, July 9, 1988.

65. Doss, *Spirit Poles*, 57.

66. Ibid., 58.

67. *Contra Costa Times*, July 9, 1988.

68. "The Concord Heritage Gateway City of Concord Begins New Era in Public Art."

69. Doss, *Spirit Poles*, 62.

70. J. H. Tompkins, "How a Good Town Gets a Bad Name," *Diablo* (August 20, 1990): 21–27.

71. *Contra Costa Times*, October 29, 1990.
72. *Contra Costa Times*, September 27, 1990.
73. *Concord Transcript*, November 22, 1989.
74. *Contra Costa Times*, March 11, 1990.
75. *Concord Transcript*, December 6, 1989.
76. *Concord Transcript*, November 22, 1989.
77. *Contra Costa Times*, October 26, 1989.
78. Quoted in Doss, *Spirit Poles*, 57.
79. *Concord Transcript*, December 6, 1989.
80. "Poles Apart: Public Art vs. the Public in Concord," *San Francisco Weekly*, December 13, 1989.
81. *Concord Transcript*, November 22, 1989.
82. *Concord Transcript*, November 8, 1989.
83. *Contra Costa Times*, November 13, 1989.
84. Ibid.
85. *Concord Transcript*, August 1, 1990.
86. Andrews, *History of Concord*, 184.
87. *Contra Costa Times*, September 25, 1960.
88. Andrews, *History of Concord*, 186.
89. *Contra Costa Times*, September 12, 1982.
90. "Todos Santos Plaza, Concord, California," *Urban Design International* 10 (1989), 3.1.
91. *Contra Costa Times*, August 11, 1988.
92. *Contra Costa Times*, February 8, 1989.
93. Ibid.
94. *Contra Costa Times*, August 11, 1988.
95. *Contra Costa Times*, January 13, 1989.
96. *Contra Costa Times*, November 21, 1988.
97. Ibid.
98. *Concord Transcript*, November 11, 1993.
99. *Concord Historical Society, Downtown Concord's Historical Walking Tour* (Concord, n.d.).
100. *Contra Costa Times*, July 9, 1987.
101. *Oakland Tribune*, September 15, 1987.
102. *Contra Costa Times*, May 18, 1994.
103. Ibid.

CONCLUSION

The culture wars continue to make headlines in the United States. America seems increasingly divided into racial, ethnic, religious, sexual, and political encampments. Analysts suggest these divisions reflect the development of fundamentally different world views among Americans. Yet this study presents a more optimistic assessment. The controversies studied here were as contentious as many current debates over religion, schools, and abortion. These conflicts reflected local tensions within cities and suburbs undergoing rapid change. Though certainly not reflective of all culture war controversies, these conflicts do urge us to consider multiple causes for current divisions rather than conclude that intractable divisions exist in American society.

As the Bay Area's population surged after World War II, the region's new transportation links drew city and suburb into a much closer relationship, allowing more residents to travel throughout the region for jobs, housing, and entertainment. Increased regional mobility tended to homogenize the metropolitan landscape. Businesses left the cities for the suburbs. "White flight" lowered urban densities and raised suburban traffic. Urban and suburban officials competed to draw regional travelers into their downtown districts. Their attempts to make outsiders feel more comfortable led to the urbanization of the suburbs and the suburbanization of the cities. In San Francisco, leaders pushed for parking garages and freeways to accommodate the suburban motorist, while BART helped create new downtowns in suburbs like Concord. As a result, cities and suburbs increasingly possessed similar forms and functions. Their convergence, however, did not bring about regional harmony. In the nineteenth century Americans viewed city and suburb as complementary environments, the city manufacturing wealth and cultural display, the suburbs providing domestic tranquility and access to nature. Today, city and suburb compete for economic power and cultural prestige. Some urbanites blame the suburbs for siphoning off central city jobs. Older suburbanites see urban development threatening their family-oriented lifestyle.

Regional mobility according to David Brodsly "frees us from the constraints of the locality," leading to "a decreased appreciation of and commitment to locality."[1] Yet, as this study has argued, many Americans remain very committed to their communities despite increased regional mobility. Neighborhood activists sought to maintain their locality's distinctiveness in the face of the transiency of communities and the convergence of city and suburb. Groups that ranged from middle-class whites to working-class minorities opposed local changes that, they argued, undermined the community's original urban or suburban identities.

Facing a region filled with rapidly growing suburbs, San Francisco leaders sought to accommodate the automobile. But freeways threatened the very essence of San Francisco's historical urban identity, leading homeowners, journalists, and others to rally to save the cable cars, the Ferry Building, and Golden Gate Park. Minority leaders in West Oakland believed that BART represented an individualistic regional culture that undermined a self-contained community. In San Jose, Chicanos opposed downtown redevelopment that used a form of local history that excised any reference to Mexican victimization to promote business growth. Finally, after BART spurred new downtown development in Concord, the city council sponsored the Heritage Gateway project that produced the "Spirit Poles" sculpture which residents protested as antithetical to the suburb's history and identity.

Ongoing regional growth and change continues to spawn new controversies. In 1990, a San Jose historic preservation committee proposed that the city commemorate U.S. army captain Thomas Fallon, who first raised the American flag at San Jose at the conclusion of the war with Mexico in 1848, and who later became the town's first mayor. The committee endorsed a bronze statue of Fallon and another man on horseback raising the American flag and decided to place the statue in downtown San Jose. The Fallon memorial drew opposition from the city's Hispanic community. They formed the Coalition to Undo Racism Effectively (CURE) and argued that the Fallon memorial celebrated the Anglo conquest of the Mexican population and the subsequent Anglo appropriation of Mexican land.[2] Other opponents simply argued that Fallon did not deserve a memorial. His small band of troops captured a deserted San Jose without firing a shot, and he only served for one year as the town's mayor. The controversy continues while the memorial remains in a warehouse.

In San Francisco another controversy linking art and ethnicity arose in 1996. Following the construction of a new Main Library, the city turned the old Main Library building over to the Asian Art Museum for its new home. The old Main Library building contained 14 murals painted on canvases by Italian artist Gottardo Piazzoni. Local historic preservationists are fighting to keep the murals in the old Main Library building. However, San Francisco's Asian American community has demanded their removal, arguing that a museum devoted to Asian art should not prominently feature works by a European artist. The Asian Art Museum has offered to pay for the removal, cleaning, and relocation of the canvases to one of the city's art museums, but the issue remains unresolved.[3]

Both controversies would raise the ire of those decrying multicultural excess. Opponents of multiculturalism would see the denigration of Capt. Fallon as evidence that no white historical figure can receive praise without the inclusion of multicultural representatives. Similarly, the inability of Asian and European art to reside within the same space would suggest the ongoing divisions in society. Proponents of multiculturalism would argue that after years of racial exclusion and cultural oppression marginalized groups are finally gaining the right to assert their influence in public design. After years of facing intolerance, why do racial minorities now have to tolerate views that perpetrate historical insults?

These questions are all relevant. But probing deeper we see that the controversies also reflect changing urban and suburban relationships. The statue, located in the central plaza, is part of the celebration of San Jose's downtown revival. The city has recently completed a new convention center, hotels, shops, repertory theater, museums, and is using art to attract visitors into the downtown.[4]

In the struggle to become a major city San Jose officials tried to increase public support for their developmental goals. They sought to use the Fallon statue to unify the population by increasing local pride. However, the statue only furthered divisions as Mexicans asserted an oppositional identity, and linked the heavy-handed attempt to force the monument onto the Mexican public as another example of the exclusion of Mexicans from the city's history and current politics.

Similarly, by building a world class Asian art museum in the city's civic center, San Francisco officials sought to confirm its role as the center of Asian culture in the Bay Area. The 1989 Loma Prieta earthquake made Oakland and San Jose more competitive for Asian American business investment. After the quake, Oakland's Asiatown boomed.[5] Thus both controversies, besides reflecting ethnic divisions, grow out of urban competition that requires city leaders to entice outside investment and visitors into their cities. City leaders increasingly promote downtown development by funding cultural projects. As minority groups grow in size they demand the right to shape the built environment, realizing that space and how it is used is an important emblem of inclusion and exclusion.

The culture wars will continue as cities and suburbs adjust to growth and change occurring within metropolitan areas. Rapid mobility means American cities and suburbs are in a constant state of construction and reconstruction. New convention centers, museums, ballparks, riverwalks, downtown malls, hotels, condominiums, and restaurants appeal to regional, national, and international visitors. City leaders use culture to spur downtown redevelopment. This heightened value and importance of culture leads to conflicts over the content of what is represented.

Mobility makes community formation and maintenance difficult. It supports an individualistic, striving lifestyle. In reaction, some residents defend local space and local identities from the transformations that certain regional connections brought. They used history to harken back to the "good old days" and saw political and business efforts to redevelop cities and suburbs as an attempt to change their original culture. New transit systems threatened to homogenize the region, bringing the total convergence of city and suburb.

When we consider new controversies as part of the culture wars we need to keep in mind that the relationship between cities and suburbs is undergoing rapid change in the U. S. Whether one views oneself as a "local" or "Black," or "Chicano," this study suggests, often depends on how the neighborhood is situated within the city, and how the city is situated within the region. While there is much analysis of the culture wars, most of it places protests within the context of national or international debates. Yet, recurring local movements challenging transportation projects and urban redevelopment should be mined for clues to evolving individual and community identities. Protests over such issues as the morality of modern art have appeared in many communities, but they do not necessarily reflect the same motivations. We should look closely at the local context in which these debates take place. We may see that they are not homogeneously debates between "orthodox" and "progressive" positions. They may reflect distinct changes taking place at the neighborhood, town, and regional levels.

NOTES

1. David Brodsley, *L.A. Freeway: An Appreciative Essay* (Berkeley, 1981), 33.
2. *San Jose Mercury-News*, June 5, 1990.
3. See *AsianWeek*, August 27, 1998; *AsianWeek*, September 10, 1998.
4. See Bruce Webber, "Cities Are Fostering the Arts As a Way to Save Downtown," *New York Times*, November 18, 1997.
5. *San Francisco Chronicle*, July 16, 1990.

BIBLIOGRAPHICAL ESSAY

In conceptualizing this book, I first familiarized myself with the many studies on the culture wars, beginning with the pioneering work by James Davison Hunter, *Culture Wars: The Struggle to Define America* (New York, 1991). Several critical essays on Hunter's culture wars concept are available in James L. Nolan, Jr., ed., *The American Culture Wars: Current Contests and Future Prospects* (Charlottesville, 1996). A good overview of the rise of the orthodox alliance is provided in Mark Gerson, *The Neoconservative Vision: From the Cold War to the Culture Wars* (Lanham, 1996). For the Left's discomfort with identity politics, see Todd Gitlin, *The Twilight of Common Dreams: Why America Is Wracked by Culture Wars* (New York, 1995). On how the Left might balance the politics of class and the politics of identity, see the first essay in Nancy Fraser, *Justice Interruptus: Critical Reflections on the "Postsocialist" Condition* (New York, 1997). For different perspectives on multiculturalism, see the collection of essays in Arthur M. Melzer, Jerry Weinberger, and M. Richard Zimman, eds., *Multiculturalism and American Democracy* (Lawrence, 1998). For criticism of identity politics and history see Arthur M. Schlesinger, Jr., *The Disuniting of America: Reflections on a Multicultural Society* (New York, 1991).

Two important works influenced my conceptualization of this study within the framework of urbanizing suburbs and suburbanizing cities: Joseph S. Wood, "Suburbanization of City Center," *Geographical Review* 78, no. 3 (July 1988): 325–329; and David M. Hummon, *Commonplaces: Ideology and Identity in American Culture* (Albany, 1990). On urbanizing suburbs, see Rob Kling, Spencer Olin, and Mark Poster, eds., *Postsuburban California: The Transformation of Orange County Since World War II* (Berkeley, 1991); and Joel Garreau, *Edge City: Life on the New*

Frontier (New York, 1991). For an insightful interpretation of urban decentralization as an expression of the urban culture of the American West, see John M. Findlay, *Magic Lands: Western Cityscapes and American Culture after 1940* (Berkeley, 1992). One should also look at other theories on urban decentralization. Greg Hise, in *Magnetic Los Angeles: Planning the Twentieth-Century Metropolis* (Baltimore, 1997), argues that industrial relocation led to the urbanization of the suburbs. For the argument that the rise of global trade helped forge suburban cities, see Peter O. Muller, "The Suburban Transformation of the Globalizing American City," *Annals of the American Academy of Political and Social Science* 551 (May 1997): 44–58. In November of 1975, the same journal devoted a whole issue to suburban urbanization (volume 422). See particularly the articles by Pierce F. Lewis, "The Galatic Metropolis," and David L. Birch, "From Suburb to Urban Place."

My focus on urban-suburban change led me to look at how transportation created a multicentered metropolis in the Bay Area. On the Bay Area's urban geography, consult James E. Vance, Jr., *Geography and Urban Evolution in the San Francisco Bay Area* (Berkeley 1964). Mel Scott, *The San Francisco Bay Area: A Metropolis in Perspective*, 2d ed. (Berkeley, 1985) is still unmatched on Bay Area city and regional planning and transportation history. For the anti-freeway movement, I consulted the extensive clipping collection at the San Francisco History Center, the main branch of the San Francisco Public Library. For the conflict over BART in West Oakland, I found the community newspaper *Flatlands* published during the mid 1960s particularly helpful. A complete run is unavailable, however scattered issues are collected in the Oakland History Room at the main branch of the Oakland Public Library. Numerous studies focus on Oakland politics during the 1960s, including Milton Viorst, *The Citizen Poor of the 1960s* (Dayton, 1977); Judith V. May, "The Struggle for Authority" (Ph.D. dissertation, University of California-Berkeley, 1973). For different perspectives on the many facets of political, social, and cultural change taking place in Oakland, see Huey P. Newton, *Revolutionary Suicide* (New York, 1973); Edward C. Hayes, *Power Structure and Urban Policy: Who Rules in Oakland?* (New York, 1971); Amory Bradford, *Oakland's Not for Burning* (New York, 1968); David L. Kirp, *Just Schools: The Ideal of Racial Equality in American Education* (Berkeley, 1982); Frank Levy, *Urban Outcomes: Schools, Streets, and Libraries* (Berkeley, 1974). For more recent political movements in San Francisco, see Richard DeLeon, *Left Coast City: Progressive Politics in San Francisco 1971-1991* (Lawrence, 1992). On the historical impact of globalism on the Bay Area, see Richard Walker, "Another Round of Globalism in San Francisco," *Urban Geography* 17, no. 1 (1996): 60–94.

My familiarity with the cultural significance of the Chicano movement gave me a critical perspective on the culture wars. The only monographic overview of the Chicano movement is Carlos Muñoz, *Youth, Identity, Power: The Chicano Movement* (London, 1989), which should be supplemented with Ramón A. Gutiérrez, "Community, Patriarchy and Individualism: The Politics of Chicano History and the Dream of Equality," *American Quarterly* 45, no. 1 (March 1993): 44–72; and Edward J. Escobar, "The Dialectics of Repression: The Los Angeles Police Department and the Chicano Movement, 1968-1971," *Journal of American History* 79 (March 1993): 1483-1514.

However, no scholar of Chicano history has made a link to urban change. This is curious since scholars of African American history often do emphasize urban transformations. For the most recent and most fruitful work, see Thomas J. Sugrue, *Origins of the Urban Crisis: Race and Inequality in Postwar Detroit* (Princeton, 1996). More has been written about Asian settlement in the suburbs. See Timothy P. Fong, *The First Suburban Chinatown: The Remaking of Monterey Park, California* (Philadelphia, 1994). However, Fong focused on inter-racial/cultural conflict as the result of changing demographics rather than the result of any change in the relationship between city and suburb.

For a treatment of pre-World War II Mexican American history that is attentive to urban geography, see George J. Sánchez, *Becoming Mexican American: Ethnicity, Culture, and Identity in Chicano Los Angeles, 1900-1945* (New York, 1993). Sánchez argues that the Mexican population was spread out in a desegregated pattern in the early 1900s, but become segregated during and after the repatriation movement of the 1930s. However, he does not continue his analysis into the 1960s. Similarly, one of the earliest and best histories of urban Mexican Americans, Albert Camarillo, *Chicanos in a Changing Society: From Mexican Pueblos to American Barrios in Santa Barbara and Southern California, 1848-1930* (Cambridge, 1980), describes how segregation helped create a strongly united population. Yet Camarillo also does not cover the 1960s.

Each separate movement within *el movimiento* now has its history, including Ignacio García, *United We Win: The Rise and Fall of La Raza Unida Party* (Tucson, 1989); Armando Navarro, *Mexican American Youth Organization: Avant-garde of the Chicano Movement in Texas* (Austin, 1995); and Armando Navarro, *The Cristal Experiment: A Chicano Struggle for Community Control* (Madison, 1998). Especially helpful on delineating the pan-Latino identity is Laurie Kay Sommers, "Inventing Latinismo: The Creation of 'Hispanic' Panethnicity in the United States," *Journal of American Folklore* 104 (1991): 32–53. For comparative purposes, see Yen Le Espiritu, *Asian American Panethnicity: Bridging Institutions and Identities* (Philadelphia, 1992).

Finally, cultural debates on modern art and American history are available in several recent studies. On art, see Erika Doss, *Spirit Poles and Flying Pigs*. On history, see Gary B. Nash, Charlotte Crabtree, Ross E. Dunn, *History on Trial: Culture Wars and the Teaching of the Past* (New York, 1997); Mike Wallace, *Mickey Mouse History and Other Essays on American Memory* (Philadelphia, 1996); Edward T. Linenthal and Tom Engelhardt, *History Wars: The Enola Gay and Other Battles for the American Past* (New York, 1996); John E. Bodnar, *Remaking America: Public Memory, Commemoration, and Patriotism in the Twentieth Century* (Princeton, 1992).

INDEX

About the Author

JOSEPH A. RODRIGUEZ is Associate Professor of History and Urban Studies at the University of Wisconsin-Milwaukee. He has published articles on the Chicano movement, urban history, and multiculturalism.

ISBN 0-275-96406-X

90000>

EAN

9 780275 964061

HARDCOVER BAR CODE